# Autonomous Art Institutions

# Autonomous Art Institutions

## Artists Disrupting the Creative City

Alberto Cossu

ROWMAN & LITTLEFIELD
*Lanham • Boulder • New York • London*

Published by Rowman & Littlefield
An imprint of The Rowman & Littlefield Publishing Group, Inc.
4501 Forbes Boulevard, Suite 200, Lanham, Maryland 20706
www.rowman.com

86-90 Paul Street, London EC2A 4NE



British Library Cataloguing in Publication Information available

Library of Congress Cataloging-in-Publication Data available

ISBN 9781786616029 (hardcover) | ISBN 9781538164303 (paperback) |
ISBN 9781786616036 (epub)

∞™ The paper used in this publication meets the minimum requirements of American National Standard for Information Sciences—Permanence of Paper for Printed Library Materials, ANSI/NISO Z39.48-1992.

*This book is dedicated to my family*

# Contents

# Acknowledgements

The reality is that this book was long overdue. It is "a suffered book" as it involved pain in meeting what I perceived were the expectations of several social institutions. The fear of being an impostor is something that we come to realise is shared across early career academics. Mark Fisher is a writer whose thoughts on the academic condition have accompanied me during the process of writing the doctoral dissertation this book draws from. Theorising from his own embodied position of suffering, he was incredibly brave to lay bare the existential pressures that affect so many of us. The pandemic has been also something that completely altered our relation to social reality. Suddenly we have no real audience, no other people with whom to make sense of the world. And yet, a shared experience of what has happened, and what is really happening, is a task that awaits us in over the next years. Intellectual debates have inundated pandemic times. What I hope this pandemic has brought to us is a fact that we thought previously unimaginable – radical world changes – became possible. This offers hope that change is possible in a short amount of time, even on a global scale. If priorities are clear, of course. If these priorities are shared, acted on. I genuinely hope that change at this scale can take place for priorities that have been left unattended for too long: environmental pollution and growing inequalities.

What is it that a sociologist does? I remember during my first year as an undergraduate hearing that sociology is a way to account for a shared social knowledge, with a specialised jargon and a privileged point of view: our social fabric. Every person has knowledge about their world, and finally, we have learned to value each one of these localised knowledges. Thanks to the influence of works such as the late Bourdieu, in which he let the subjects speak, and systematically, in the work of Pierre de Certeau, we have learned to appreciate knowledge from the margins of society. The every day already provides us with a wealth of knowledge on society, and sociology has learned to be implicated with the processes, but never losing its adherence to a shared standard. This means that I am myself a social subject implicated on so many levels in this research. I have undertaken a journey about artists' political engagement with many allies, friends and colleagues.

I wish to thank Carolina, for without her this book would have never existed. Her constant support, inspiration and, yes, also pragmatism has made this book real and, most importantly, my life meaningful. My family has been the pillar of my academic journey, and their love and support has made me feel curious and open about the world. My infinite gratitude to you, Beatrice, Efisio and Ilaria.

I am indebted to the many people who made my academic journey possible, starting from my supervisor at the University of Milan, Adam Arvidsson. So much more than a supervisor, an accomplice, a friend and an intellectual, from which I have learned the craft of the job and the pleasure of doing research. Thanks to Adam also for creating a group of scholars from which I have learned so much: Massimo Airoldi, Davide Beraldo, Alessandro Caliandro, Alessandro Gandini and Vincenzo Luise. In Milan I was part of a PhD cohort with whom I have shared so many classes and anxieties about our doctoral journey, among them a special thanks to Maitrayee Deka, Marcello Natili and Valeria Piro. Last but not least, I would like to thank my second supervisor, Roberta Sassatelli, with whom I have had fundamental conversations about my thesis and the PhD coordinator, Luisa Leonini: the opportunities I have had at the Graduate School in social and political studies has been the ideal platform from which I could start my career.

I am also deeply grateful to our PLANK collective, that I co-founded with Marc Allen Herbst, Jessica Holtaway and Paula Serafini. The conference we organised at King's College on Art, Labour, and Activism in 2015 was central to my journey. We then embarked on editing a book on these topics that was published by Rowman & Littlefield. A special thanks to the editors with whom I have worked so far: Scarlet Furness, Frankie Mace, Gurdeep Mattu and Emma Parfitt. It was a pleasure working with you, and I hope there is more to come. Also, I take the chance to thank Athina Karatzogianni for her support, scholarship and inspiration at the University of Leicester.

Thanks to the wonderful co-authors with whom I have developed some of the work presented in this book. While I acknowledge their contributions, I also wish to take full responsibility for the outcome. Maria Francesca Murru, Marianna d'Ovidio, I was lucky to count on your expertise when it came to craft my first academic papers. Thank you.

I am deeply indebted to Macao, for their generosity, for having created such an inspiring vision. I am not sure I could do justice to the complexity of Macao, and I hope there will be more shared projects in the future.

Among them I wish to express my deepest gratitude to Emanuele Braga, Manuela Casiraghi, Angelo Castucci, Luca Chiaudano, Cristina Fiordimela, Maddalena Fragnito, Ferdinando Mazzitelli, Camilla Pin and Diego Weisz. Thanks for your trust and friendship. I wish to express a special thought for a brave man who surprised me so many times. I will always remember our last chat in Porta Venezia, discussing the fine details of the political power of memetic left. Ciao, Corra.

# Introduction

This book is about artists and creative workers that attempt to create new conditions for art, cultural production and society at large. Involved in the main struggles of their time, they have become a fundamental voice in the debates that surround alternative economies and new organisational forms in the artistic and creative sector. They have done so also seeking a new dialectic with the cities they inhabit. This book draws from an ethnography that I conducted from May 2012 to January 2015, and then for another stint from April 2016 to January 2018 where I took part in some projects hosted by Macao. This book is largely based on the ethnography of Macao, the New Center for Arts, Culture and Research of Milan (Italy). Macao officially started on 5 May 2012 and the book will trace a detailed genealogy of its emergence up until the point it now can be defined as an Autonomous Art Institution.

I have been an ethnographer and a researcher within the university for which I was preparing a doctoral dissertation, but as also a researcher that was directly involved in the struggles of artists and creatives. I have participated in numerous projects, giving my contribution as I was learning what it means for this generation of artists to be involved in political and social matters. On my Facebook profile, under rubric past employments, one could read that I was a 'former researcher at Macao'. Interesting debates have examined to what level our platformed lives can be interpreted as 'real'. In this sense, I have actively contributed to projects as an external collaborator, as a friendly supporter and also a co-creator. This happened in projects such as the inquiry conducted within the 2015 Milan Expo and, the following year, a co-developed consultancy on the festival of Santarcangelo, one of the major performing arts festivals in Italy.

It might be said that this kind of research is in line with the established lineage of *militant* and co-research, and that lineage would surely capture a part of what has happened during my research process. However, I believe the most important thing is to provide knowledge that is useful for understanding the social reality for both the academic audience and the furthering of progressive causes in our society. During the extensive collaborations that took place during my fieldwork (2012–2015) and afterwards (2016–2018), one overarching issue was finding a good ethical stance for this double role in the academic and activist field. I have tried to navigate and provide a sound rationale for this in the methodological chapter. My relationship with Macao is based on gratitude, co-belonging and has been forged in the debates I have conducted in the numerous academic conferences, in which I have presented my scholarly work. What I have learned so far is that one fundamental reason for which a PhD student – such as the one I was in the early 2010s – could have sympathy for a critique put forth by artists, creatives and knowledge workers as they did was due to Macao representing many of the stances that resonated with the precarious conditions of early career researchers. This is an intellectual habit that I have learned via the tradition of critical sociology and the heritage of *con-ricerca* – co-research, also known as worker's inquiry, theorised by Romano Alquati (see Bedani and Ioannilli 2020) – referring to practices of critically engaged research that, among other things, puts into brackets the differences in social status to find a fundamental solidarity, a solidarity beyond the value that a certain social system assigns to subjects (e.g., academics, artists, technicians, etc.).

Ultimately, what you will find in the following pages is an ethnographic rendition and a theoretical analysis of *three key phases* in the life of Macao. The first phase investigates the spark that led this political mobilisation of artists to come into being, the second is represented by the organisational patterns that emerge in the ensuing years, while the third establishes what kind of relationship this wave of art activism means for urban governance. The book closes with a reflection on the desire to create an alternative art institution.

Unlike my original PhD thesis, which forms the backbone of this text – I hope this will not be felt too cumbersome – my attempt here is to keep the original richness of this topic, while ensuring higher readability for a wider audience. Finally, it features a new and broader introduction that you are reading now and an extended concluding chapter in which I present and reflect on the last lines of work steered not only by Macao but by a wider movement that is connected with digital governance innovation and blockchain-based alternative economies.

What I hope this book can be is a vivid, detailed account of how a group of Italian artists and creatives have sought to create an Autonomous Art Institution. This book places my scholarly work and the doings of Macao in a wider frame that is capable to better theorise aspects that, in the first instance, relate to the *debate on art and activism*. It is crucial to situate the activities of artistic activism within the struggles and the issues of *creative work*. I will bridge the existing findings with these new parts by thickening a strand that was only running underneath in my dissertation. This narrative thread relates to the notion of *institution* that describes the attempt of stabilisation of an art-activists' movement whose aim has been to deliberately create a stable organisation to fulfil their aims. The notion of the institution is explored theoretically in the introduction and the conclusion while, in the core chapters of the book, it is explored via the concept of *event*. It might seem paradoxical to put the concept of institution and event next to each other, but in the doings of artistic practice, it is precisely through ruptures that can be interpreted via the concept of the event that we can reach a fuller understanding of the trajectory that takes us from a mobilisation to an institution.

## BEYOND DIALECTIC: THE POLITICAL POWER OF THEORISING A NEW SUBJECT

This book explores the endeavours of a group of artists and creatives in a well-defined urban space: the city of Milan. This city is a major centre for the Italian economy and a productive region with many high-added-value industries such as fashion, architecture and design. It is also a city that is currently perceived as a capital of the most advanced industries in services and design, a hub in line with global trends that have been observed across many cities (Zukin 1989). This is coupled with a historical migration that in the post-war era saw mostly migrants from the south of Italy move to Northern industrial regions. Some of these migrants would then become a new force in worker's movements, changing completely the attitude towards traditional unions and parties, for they appeared much more autonomous (Tarrow 1989) vis-à-vis what they perceived as an institutional political system incapable of dealing with their issues. In this sense, to borrow the original subtitle of *The Golden Horde* – written by Nanni Balestrini and Primo Moroni and one of the most important books to address the workers' struggles from 1960 to 1977 in Italy – it was a great 'revolutionary, creative, political and existential wave'. The misalignment among the autonomy of these new post-workerist workers resonates with the conditions experienced by later generation of activists, including the ones that we are discussing in this book. Or, in a similar vein, theorising the emergence of a new class of workers is the foundation of understanding implied in the notion of 'social worker' (*operaio sociale*). In Negri's famous book '*Marx Beyond Marx*' (1992) which the English translation of the book claims is possibly 'the greatest contribution to Marxism, ever', he problematises Marx's dialectic approach. Negri affirms he led Marx's contradictions, based on antagonism, to explode. The *operaio sociale* is a historical subject on the cusp of fulfilling a long lineage of antagonism and yet, the dissolution of capitalism's dialectic.

This is also visible in the ways in which I have understood Macao's internal political attitude as being a-dialectic or post-dialectic: unwilling to struggle on an uneven field maintained by backward parties and unions, more willing to affirm their own potency in a positive way. In this sense, I have come to believe that to situate Macao in a political and cultural history one has to return to the roots of a new subjectivity that was first diagnosed in the 1960s and 1970s in the post-workerist canon pioneered by the works of Antonio Negri. In his book, Negri (1992) theorises a capacity of self-valorisation which is autonomous, coming to see the subject as a bearer of an absolute constituent power. This is the ultimate foundation, often vindicated as the heritage of a new generation of activists that recognise the generation of Negri, and the ones in the *Autonomy,* a capacity to express the capacity of a multitude of subjects to self-determination.

This calls for an assessment of the performative role that theories have in providing meaning, scope and architecture to activist practices. It is noteworthy that many issues surrounding art and immaterial labour, such as precarity, that we find resurfacing in many debates, were organised in 2008 at the Tate Britain, and hosted the key theorists of post-workerism, including Franco Berardi 'Bifo', Maurizio Lazzarato, Antonio Negri and Judith Revel. Official documentation of these debates is included in the book curated by Peter Osborne and Eric Alliez (2013). On the other hand, anthropologist David Graeber offered a poignant account on the roles these theorists have had in shaping activist waves in his piece 'The sadness of post-workerism' (Graeber 2008):

> At this point I think I can return to my initial question: why does one need a revolutionary philosopher to help us think about art? Why does one call in a prophet? The answer would appear to be: One calls in a prophet because prophets above all know how to speak compellingly about their audience's place in history. Certainly this is the role in which Negri, Bifo, and the rest have now been cast. They have become impresarios of the historical moment. When their ideas are invoked by artists or philosophers, this is largely what those artists and philosophers seem to be looking for. When they are brought on stage at public events, this is mainly what is expected of them. Their job is to explain why the time we live in is unique, why the processes we see crystallizing around us are unprecedented; different in quality, different in kind, from anything that has ever come before. (Graeber 2008, 14)

Graeber in his account of this pivotal conference uses the term 'prophet' to describe the unique quality of the political endeavour of these theorists.

In my case, I explore the dynamics of this relationship in different parts of the book. It is explicitly theorised in the first chapter when I discuss the role deliberative democracy had on social movements, furthermore, it is acknowledged in ethnographic accounts of the intellectuals that interacted with and inspired Macao.

## MILAN: THE TALE OF A CREATIVE CITY

Today, Milan hosts ambitious youth that come from the whole of Italy to work in many of their industries. Mostly, recent researchers (see Mattoni 2012, for a review) have concentrated on workers being exploited in the creative industries and this is also connected to the recent history of political mobilisations against precarity in these industries. Particularly relevant is the case of May Day, which in Milan since the early 2000s came to represent a parade for the rights of atypical workers, rather than the established ones that are usually celebrated by Unions in Rome on 1 May.

Milan is a city with a long and rich history of contentious politics, social movements and unrest. This is because it was at the epicentre of a form of industrialism whose critique in the 1960s and 1970s was most heavily felt. It was a pioneer in the transition to the service economy and currently to the digital economy. Chapter 5 of this book is devoted entirely to the discussion of the relationship between artistic critique and the neoliberal city. This heritage is also felt in the customs of artistic criticism that saw the neighbourhood of Isola (in the West of Milan) hosting alternative points of view to the ones offered by the New York artist/architect Gordon Matta-Clark. In two residencies between 1973 and 1975, he created artworks titled *Infraform* that consisted of triangular cuts on the concrete walls of abandoned industrial buildings in the Isola, creating new perspectives on these buildings. These were then joined by anti-gentrification efforts led by the Isola Art Center, founded by the Luxembourg-born artist Bert Theis, who was also a teacher at NABA (*Nuova Accademia di Belle Arti*, New Academy of Fine Arts) and inspirator for many of the co-founders of Macao.

Universities and *Accademie* in Milan played a pivotal role in all these processes, as they have been implicated in the education of many, if not most, of the creative and knowledge workers that later tried to find alternatives to a life made of unpaid internships and underpaid labour in the creative industries, notably in fashion. Milan hosts seven large universities, and eleven *Accademie* that span photography, art, fashion, product design, new media, and so on. Most of them 'produce' creatives that seek to integrate themselves in the existing paradigm/model and some physiologically either create alternatives or join the ranks of those that seek to establish a new paradigm in the sector.

Macao initially appears in 2012 as a not-so-identifiable entity in the city. In fact, the surprise was large among those who witnessed the emergence and the eruption of Macao in the city of Milan. A comment I would usually get from colleagues and friends in those days insisted on the same refrain that went: 'this does not look like an Italian kind of protest; this seems like a Berlin protest'. Looking at the international standing of the city of Milan, and the fact that some of its founders have considerable international experience, at that point some fled after the trauma of the 2001 G7 protests and repression in Genoa, some others sought a better livelihood in the art sector in cities such as Berlin or in countries such as Belgium, famous for its welfare for European artists and creatives. This was also coupled with a general trend in decreased public spending for arts and culture that has been observed in Italy for at least twenty years.

During my ethnography, I came to realise that the squatting culture, to which Macao can be ascribed to, was made of varied elements that mixed the Italian tradition of antagonist *Centri Sociali* (Occupied Social Centres) along with elements imported from the Northern European tradition, and in particular Germany and the Netherlands (Pruijt 2004, 2013; Moore 2015). This can also be seen as a relevant bricolage between the memory of past struggles (Zamponi 2018) and the incorporation of tendencies that valorise 'best' activist practices where they emerge. This process, however, does not happen all the time, and this was especially evident when during the global affirmation of the Occupy movement, Italians did not occupy. As to why this did not happen, I will point you in the direction of the excellent analysis put forth by Zamponi (2012) in which he hypothesises that it was mainly due to the coincidence of the capacity of the then prime minister Silvio Berlusconi to attract a malaise that had wider and deeper referents – the EU imposed austerity in the post-2008 financial crisis – and the movements failed to rebuild after a loss of credibility due to rioting and the widespread internal fractures in their coalition.

Numerous links connect Macao and its wave of protest with larger and broader scenarios. In the next section, I will illustrate a series of concentric circles that explore these different connections and interdependencies.

## SITUATING MACAO IN A BROADER CONTEXT

The most obvious network is the one created by artists themselves from 2010 onwards across Italy, with mixed success, and very different time spans and relevance. This is discussed in depth in chapters 3, 4 and 5, but I would like to underline how this mobilisation starts with a specific focus on performing arts, a sector in crisis, founding the Network of 'Occupied Theatres' in 2011. Macao joins in 2012, from Milan, occupying an abandoned skyscraper in the heart of its business district. This reflects the different compositions, priorities and also the level of development of a creative sector in the city of Milan when compared to other Italian cities. In this sense, the mobilisation of Macao connects avant-garde elements drawn from previous artistic practices and international influences expanding beyond an exclusively sectorial preoccupation for the performing arts to a larger struggle for the right to the city. The predecessors of these movements were *Centri Sociali*, alternative spaces that emerged in Italy during the 1980s and 1990s. Mostly, discussions on these places revolved around their role in social inclusion, alternative cultural production as in the case of self-produced rap music in the 1990s (Mathieu and Balasinski 2006). Culturally and politically antagonist, when placed in the wider social context, these spaces have been viewed as placing themselves in a sort of 'ghetto' (Moroni et al. 1995).

In the last five years in Italy, there has been considerable hype around the idea of 'new cultural institutions' led by grassroots organisations. Unlike formal institutions, they see cultural production as something to be re-appropriated from the activities that take place in the private sector and in the third sector (voluntary and community organisations). Using approaches that have had mixed fortune in recent times as social innovation, commoning and public art. This scene is composite and includes private foundations sponsoring open calls to support the creation of innovative projects that generally see culture and art in a close relationship with social and cultural issues. cheFare, an agency for 'cultural transformation' based in Milan, has been pivotal in this process by funding and creating a shared discourse with its main stakeholders – local institutions, academics, artists, practitioners. As we will see in the methodological chapter (see figure 2.2), cheFare represents a key broker that acts as a junction point among more radical projects and established institutions. Overall, this testifies a change in the focus, for which culture and art in Italy were often conflated in the dimension of heritage to be preserved as part of Italian excellence.

Macao's cultural relevance is also indicated by an intense intellectual production that has flourished. Many scholars and researchers from across the globe have collaborated with Macao on different levels, from contributing to seminars to writing pieces on Macao. Many students from Milan, Sheffield, Amsterdam and other cities have spent some time doing research on Macao, ultimately compiling dozens of theses about it. Artistic institutions, including the ZKM in Karlsruhe and the Reina Sofia Museum, have ongoing collaborations with Macao or individual artists within it. Free software advocates such as Richard Stallman have been hosted there, along with radical cryptocurrency designers that have been pivotal in nurturing a conversation that for Macao, as well for many other similar spaces, has been crucial for the prospects of creating alternative financial viability as well as trying to rethink the idea of value in a contemporary economy.

The Italian network of occupied theatres, and most notably Teatro Valle in Rome, hosted countless debates that saw eminent scholars, from Stefano Rodotà and Ugo Mattei – pioneers in the discussion on commons in Italy – to David Harvey, hosted during three days of events in 2012. It would be impossible to list them all, and, surely, I am not doing justice to the richness and diversity of these debates. In this sense, this work also demonstrates a limitation in how a scholar can render the complexity of not just a single space, or a network of spaces, but a whole cultural and political movement that has so many ramifications and intricacies.

Macao has many facets, and in this wave of activism, these aspects include important debates that are an integral part of this wave. And I am aware these are not adequately covered in the book. I wish here to point towards some of these debates that are extremely fruitful in advancing new ways of producing change on so many levels. For instance, there has been a decisive focus on feminism, especially taken from a wide angle of transfeminism and queer approaches. This was dealt with in Macao via seminars and weekly meetings in which the aim was to establish an open culture of non-discrimination, also in the attempt to hijack the residual elements of patriarchy and to produce a joyful, non-normative view. In this area, activists from Macao have built alliances with critical scholars and makers to engage with practices and theories of care (The Care Collective 2020) and the issue of repair (Graziano and Trogal 2019). A reflexive take that sees care as a viable path to redefine lives, cities, workplaces and activist spaces.

## FROM ART ACTIVISM TO AUTONOMOUS ART INSTITUTIONS

When I think of art, images of paintings, museums, sculptures come to my mind. In particular, I remember when I was a student doing my undergraduate studies. I encountered the first prominent example of art that was intended to have a social relevance. A professor of mine talked us through the meaning of a magnificent fresco in Siena's medieval town hall that dates to flourishing communal times. The author of the painting is Ambrogio Lorenzetti, and the uber-famous fresco represents allegories of *Buon Governo e Cattivo Governo* (The Allegory of Good and Bad Government). Quentin Skinner famously theorised on this fresco, envisioning the capacity of an artist to act being no less than a political philosopher (Skinner 1986). If I think back on it now, I am surprised by how perfectly the fresco links with my present questions about the current developments of contemporary art. In the first place, because Lorenzetti's work is powerfully and willingly (a hermeneutic perspective would also suggest: unavoidably) rooted to the political and institutional spirit of the time, it embodies and channels a newly constituted social order based on autonomous *Comuni* – the Communes or city-states that developed in central and northern Italy since the twelfth century – that claimed and needed new representations. Lorenzetti received the commission of the fresco from the recently established ruling class (the so-called *Nove*, as they were nine, exactly the same number of wedges of the *Campo* square that hosts the Palazzo in front of it). *Nove* were a guild of merchants that took over the city of Siena and governed it from 1287 to 1355. The artist, in this case Lorenzetti, did more than just paint a received wisdom or official religious themes. He painted political ideals with brush strokes rather than words, an ideal that interestingly resurged in political and economic ideals quite recently: the common good is the supreme good and should be elevated to the position of the ruler if a government wants to ensure peace and prosperity.[1] Apart from economic and political considerations on this historical shift, the echoes of recent thinking on the commons as the main alternative to the capitalist system (Hess and Ostrom 2011) will resound in chapters 4 and 5. I would like to draw the attention to three themes that are key to my intervention.

In the first place, art allows us to inspect a historical fracture that has produced a different kind of art, reflecting a rupture in the cultural imagination of that time that was (and socially speaking, had to be) represented in the fresco. This anchor could also lead us to further investigations on temporality, and regimes of historicity. In this sense, our focus is about placing oneself on the side of continuity or on the side of genealogies of history as built by ruptures that make different times incommensurable before and after an event occurs (Sewell 1996). Second, art allows us to witness a moment in which a new institution arises. In the case of *Comuni*, it was a success and it was capable to inspire a fruitful legacy in terms of thought and governing principles. Finally, the cultural needs commanded by the existence of a new institutional setting demand that a certain number of artefacts adequately display and influence the surroundings of such a novel space. This is the realm of influence, and spans from Lorenzetti's fresco that (according to the aesthetic principles of the time) should have inspired and guided the decisions taken by the nine magistrates by the simple fact of being imposed over their heads, on the walls in which they united to deliberate.

If this trans-historic parallel is founded, then this book can be seen as a new instance of a long story, a tale of how a new class (the art workers) has struggled and is struggling to gain power (as the *Nove* struggled against medieval forces), producing artefacts that enabled them to finally attempt to create institutions that could survive them and ultimately become the seeds of a society to come.

The changes in both art and politics since the Middle Ages have been conspicuous, and there has been a major break in modern times. Kant and Schiller are credited for theorising an autonomous space for artistic activity clearly separated from the drudgery of labour and the indulgence of aristocracy. In this sense, art must be free from the constraints that normally apply. An exercise in virtuosity that allows an artist to be self-valorising, not taking into account the measures of value and worth from without. Later on, after revolutions, the abolishment of empires, the creation of republics and the reform of absolute powers, we reach the twentieth century where the picture starts to complexify considerably. The reflections of Walter Benjamin about aesthetics and politics during Nazi Fascism remind us at once of art's power and how it can be a problematic form for the legitimisation of power. The Futurist movement in Italy is known for having walked hand in hand with Fascists in the early days (and more!). Mass and rapid industrialisation has also called for groups to look back at the traditional ways of creating things, if we consider the Arts and Craft movement. A certain kind of *engagé* art – although Guy Debord would certainly disagree – has been a part of the 1968 struggles.[2]

What is most pressing here is the question of art's autonomy, especially if we consider how, in recent times, artists have become ethnographers (the observation of human culture). Going back to the concerns that Benjamin voiced in 1934 (see Foster 1995), it has been debated if the object of artistic transformation should be the site of political transformation – an otherness to which the artist has access to a citizen of our society and as artist. The risk here is one of the ideological patronage of causes that are beyond the direct remit of artists' own concerns. If this was the case and artists empowered or instrumentalised struggles that belonged to other social groups (the proletariat, the labourers, ethnic minorities, etc.) what we witness today is their claim, from the left, that artists and creatives have been a part of society since their inception and that they are subjected to similar structural forces as other groups. In this sense, many groups – from *Intermittents* in France, French art workers, to the wave of art activism sparked in the last decade – have sought to destroy the myth of the pacified artist of Kantian memory: normally trained in liberal arts schools, contributors who, with the grace of their talent, symbolise a reality outside the realm of politics.

Another dividing line separates professionally trained artists and the 'folk' creativity that has been used by activists during protests. This has constituted a foundational theoretical cleavage to distinguish between the field in which activists employ creativity and artistic means to protest and demonstrate from the field in which artists redefine the meaning and the scope for art itself as it dissolves in social and economic processes. By recurring to a notion of 'folk' creativity, I am also referring to a cleavage that separates it from avant-garde, in both artistic and political terms. A similar distinction has been pivotal in the critique made by Srnicek and Williams (2016) about the waves of political unrest that took place in the last ten years, and also structurally resembles the distinction between high and popular culture.

As it appears in the history of Macao, artistic legitimation comes from new and old art academies, and yet in being subjects of history embedded in the creative industries makes them political subjects first and foremost. This is a claim to reshuffle priorities since their artistic will is exerted in the denial of performing the artists' role in a pacified way. In this respect, what we know from a shared view on artists' position in society is that it appears to respond to a paradigm that has seen only minimal changes across decades. Following Menger's analysis:

> Artists as an occupational group are on average younger than the general work force, are better educated, tend to be more concentrated in a few metropolitan areas, show higher rates of self-employment, higher rates of unemployment and of several forms of constrained underemployment (non-voluntary part-time work, intermittent work, fewer hours of work), and are more often multiple job holders. They earn less than workers in their reference occupational category, that of professional, technical and kindred workers, whose members have comparable human capital characteristics (education, training and age), and they experience larger income inequality and variability. (Menger 2001, 242)

Artists' position in society points to a condition that is far from being contextual or episodic. The uncertainty faced by artists is structural for the sector globally, and the creative city (Florida 2002) is not a solution to this problem, it rather exacerbates the contradictions of this unbalance. This fact constitutes the main underpinning that explains the explosion of activism in this sector. As I also discuss in chapter 5, one could also interpret this wave of activism as an instrumental form to resolve some work-related issues. Activism then can result in an accumulation of social capital that can mitigate the toughness of the job market. However, this is not an easy fix, since being an activist comes with strong demands about what it means to meet an ideal image of an 'engaged artist as activist'. I discuss this at length in chapter 4.

What is then at stake when in order to come to terms with the social, cultural and economic juncture artists and creative desire to create new institutions? And how should we grasp this? On a philosophical level, it is about theorising the possibility for subjects to modify the conditions of their existence. As we discussed earlier, on a metaphysical vein, it is about attributing the subject with a surplus of agency. But on what level exactly is this creation placed? If viewed from the inside of the art field, we could be tempted to inscribe it in a self-referential loop in which the creation of institutions is a sabotage/situationist approach. This could be the case for 'artificial institutions' (Sholette 2016), which can also be connected to the ways in which Fluxus, a creative community, established artistic production to resemble a corporation (Dumett 2018).

To disentangle the intricate web of desires, needs and possibilities tied up in an artistic movement we might ask: Why should artists create new institutions, or claim that their collectives should be viewed as such? From a sociological angle, we understand institutions as structures that embed and establish values and practices. Following Durkheim's classical account, institutions are created in moments of social effervescence, and they symbolise the sacredness and durability of a social bond. In a process of increased social differentiation, new institutions arise as they signal shifts in the social fabric. Institutes for workers' welfare clearly testify a path that has started from local mutualist associations in the nineteenth century that later reached an institutionalisation within modern states. But this institutionalisation seems at odds with the alterity (state of otherness) and the prejudicial distrust that marginal groups (if compared to the centrality of the state) hold towards institutions. Ultimately is the need to create alternative, autonomous institutions connected to the shortcomings of existing institutions – parties and unions – to represent the interests of creatives and artists? This also calls for a difference between representation and action. We can fix this conundrum by separating the realms in which this happens. It is precisely a distrust towards a representation that fuels the need to make and create their own alternative. Institutions should also be apprehended in a context in which the notion of the institution has been deeply embedded in the art world. Art institutions have been discussed in debates on new institutionalism as a new wave of curatorial attitude emerged in Europe in the 1990s. The aim was to change the artistic institution from the inside making it an open and inclusive space for cultural and artistic debate. This was also influenced by the rise of what Bourriaud defines as 'relational aesthetics' (Bourriaud 2002), incorporating a wider range of human and social relations within artistic institutions to move beyond the self-referentiality of art. In this sense, the idea is to produce a superficial paradox in which institutions are thought of as rigid units whose limitations are solved by providing 'new' art institutions with a capacity to be crossed by open flows and remain malleable and porous. Such a relational turn has created a sustained debate for years (Bishop 2012; Kester 2011). Bishop problematised the relationship between artworks, participatory practices and the institutions that promote it, stressing more on the ethical rather than artistic quality of such projects, displacing the level on which they should be understood. On the other hand, Kester surveyed a number of artistic collectives and projects across the world, noting how after the institutionally led relational turn, artists have started to intervene in the activities of NGOs, activists and urban planners. Accordingly, there is still a part that is left out from this picture: when artists themselves become activists, dissolving their own art in an art project that includes becoming an institution. And that is exactly what this book tackles.

## CHAPTER OUTLINE

This book tries to grasp this process of becoming an institution by relying on a theoretical framework that reflects my intellectual journey, along with its turns and twists. It takes an eclectic approach and also bears the origin of this book in the form of a PhD thesis organised around chapters that have a degree of autonomy. This theoretical mix considers debates in social movement studies, deliberative democracy, media studies, organisational studies, urban sociology, along with debates on the creative city. Overall, however, I believe this book could be better understood as a sociology book based on ethnography and digital methods that deploy numerous concurring perspectives in the attempt to do justice to the complexity of a phenomenon. The chapters also reflect a temporal continuity that moves from the inception of Macao in 2012 following its activities until 2015. In the conclusion, I offer an account of what Macao has achieved since having had sufficient resources to think of itself as an institution in a more accomplished manner.

This book appropriates Macao as an excellent prism through which to investigate the everyday political work carried out by artists. In doing so, my aim is to overcome the instrumental view that is often applied to art and aesthetics in the context of protest: seeing them as colourful tools to gain visibility and secure recruitment. In my work, I highlight how art might take unexpected forms in political activity, forms that are rarely embodied in the artefacts we are normally used to. Art is capable of running deep below the perceivable surface to connect and innervate the flows that circulate in a number of different media.

The book is divided into two main parts: the first comprises chapters 1 and 2 and sets the frame in which I situate my work, introducing debates around artists' political involvement (chapter 1, Framing Art and Political Mobilisation) and presenting the methodological framework (chapter 2, Behind-the-Scenes: An Ethnography of Artists). The second part is made up of three chapters (chapter 3, 4 and 5) that explore what I have come to identify as the main areas of Macao's activity: action, relation and production. The first of these three chapters (chapter 3, Art's Own Activism) deals with the logic of action, in which I stress how an artistic sensitivity was deeply embedded in the first spectacular events that granted Macao wide and favourable national and international exposure: what I have defined as an 'eventful logic'. The second (chapter 4, Organising Being an Institution) explores the theme of organisation, a key area of the political intervention of Macao activists, in which a reflexive desire for instability is coupled with surprising efficiency and the inversion of the traditional equation through which organisational forms become transient configurations determined by the eventfulness of their routine activity. The third chapter (chapter 5, Producing Culture in the Neoliberal City) investigates Macao's models of artistic and cultural production. The case is explored with the aim of understanding to what extent Macao, and in general the global wave of art activism, constitutes an alternative to the neoliberal articulation of the creative city in Milan. On the one hand, I ask whether Macao is a political actor able to influence local cultural policy and to what extent it is included in the urban governance of Milan. On the other hand, I argue that Macao is not only an actor included in urban governance, but it also provides the city a different cultural offer: open to bottom-up processes.

The three core chapters, although partially autonomous, present a *fil rouge* (red thread), which coincides with the hypothesis that a broader change in terms of social and economic critique is taking place at a global level. As processes like the eventification and the brandisation of culture represent some of the most efficient capitalist devices they now come to be appropriated in critical terms by probably the most skilled and apt subjects for a change: artists, and, more generally, cultural workers. Often trained at prestigious education institutions within the creative industry, their critique deploys the knowledge they have paid to obtain and attempts not just to antagonise political processes but to create a real and viable alternative.

The book closes with concluding remarks (chapter 6) on the significance of these processes on a wider scale, along with a systematisation of the different roles art has in political processes.

I hope you will enjoy it.

## *Chapter 1*

# Framing Art and Political Mobilisation

Within the field of sociology, a crisis of democracy seems to be occurring at the present time (Crouch 2004; Dalton 2004; Held 2006; Gray and Caul 2000; Formenti 2010; Putnam 2000; Rosanvallon 2006; Todd 2008). The literature, although originating from different perspectives, underscores a legitimacy and representation deficit in our present democratic systems. At a national level, in particular, the literature illuminates peculiar anomalies of the Italian political system that shows, on the one hand, a globally underdeveloped civil society profoundly differentiated along the north-south axis (Banfield 1958; Cartocci 2007; Putnam 1993; Sabatini 2005) and, on the other hand, a political/institutional system colonised by the party system. Such anomalies must be considered in association with various symptoms which globally affect democratic systems: the emergence of sub-politics (Beck 1992), the reduction of nation-state sovereignty (e.g. strategic issues in favour of supranational institutions[1]), the transformation of political mass parties into *cartel parties* (Katz and Mair 1995) – the interpenetration of party and state, a pattern of inter-party collusion – and the loss of labour unions. According to Crouch (2004), we are living in *post-democratic* political systems in which – despite formal democratic institutions legitimated by elections – there is a progressive weakening of the legitimacy of policies and politics.[2] Furthermore, the recent global economic crisis which started in 2008 more acutely rendered the consequences of neoliberal capitalism,[3] not only for the traditionally weaker subjects in society but also for the middle classes. In such a context of increasing social and economic inequalities,[4] a number of actors in civil society[5] are standing up and protesting.

Since the late 1990s, a large number of social movements have reached the public stage. For analytical purposes, these can be separated into three main strands, according to their organisational form and the political culture they embody. The first strand considers the experiences that can be grouped under the heading of the Global Justice Movement. Throughout the last decade hundreds of national or local movements, both virtually and physically, joined a network whose most visible embodiments have been the World and European Social Forums. Their political stances have become less radical and increasingly reformist; apart from the more or less colourful parades they have staged and the episodes of violence in which these movements have been involved during the years. The political action of promoters and enactors of practices inspired by deliberative democratic ideals (della Porta 2005) aims to reform the current institutional edifice without calling into question its foundations. They envisage through their practices, a galaxy of bottom-up, grassroots processes as the only solution to legitimise, and to bring about 'real' democracy to a nation or a supranational institution – that transcends national boundaries or government.

A second strand of social movements, much more recent and at once politically close and organisationally distant from the first, is the wave of indignation sparked by the Arab Spring in late 2010 and early 2011. This network of movements, according to notable scholars (Bennett and Segerberger 2012; Castells 2012), showed how social media allowed the emergence of new patterns of organisation. A network infrastructure does not just facilitate and render incommensurably lower the cost of getting in contact to connect and organise movements, but has rendered formal organisations obsolete. In this context, formal organisations (unions, student associations, NGOs and various civil society actors) – bearers of the traditional *collective* logic – did not play a relevant role in Occupy or Indignados movements[6] which embody a different, *connective* logic.

At any rate, Castells' (2012) insightful analysis regarding the indignation wave allows us to trace a political continuity between this wave and previous movements. Concerning, particularly, the Western cases of the Occupy movement in the United States and the Indignados in Spain – beyond a strong moralistic opposition to the inefficiencies of the ruling class in Spain or intolerable North American policies in favour of the 1 per cent – we can witness a certain appeal given to bottom-up, deliberative practices. This appeal to consensus has, more recently, caused violent reactions within the Occupy movement itself, as is clearly shown by the article that appeared in February 2013 on Occupy Wall Street's official website, which stated:

> Consensus process is the tyranny of the individual. It is the most anti-social of all processes because it allows any one person to assert irrational authority over an entire group of people and block any sort of decision making. It has nothing do with anarchism (even the IWW doesn't use consensus!) because it was invented by Quakers for religious reasons. It's stood in the way of progress,

> destroyed social movements, destroyed groups, destroyed communities, and relegated radicals to the fringes of American politics since the 70s when it was first popularized.[7]

Notwithstanding the intrinsic civic value of such events, and acknowledging their merits and the innovations they are capable of bringing about, the thorough enquiry into their values and ideals conducted by Castells and his team allows us to see that they represent a political continuity, at least concerning their content. In a nutshell, they agree with the current institutional setting, they advocate more participation without putting into question the merits or demerits of representative democracy, and they condemn the perversion of financial-capitalism without questioning the capitalist system itself.[8]

We could use, by stretching it a little, the concept of 'undivisiveness' elaborated by Mauro Barisione (2009) for postmodern political candidates, to refer to the dynamics of such movements. According to Barisione, such candidates have 'a generic and fundamentally non-partisan character: no core socio-political cleavages are evoked and no zero-sum policy solutions are emphasised in the campaign's communication strategy' (Barisione 2009, 50). Although the analogy might seem outrageous to some readers, the '99% against the elitist 1%' frame proposed by Occupy is limited as it did not actually make it possible to grasp real political cleavages.

The third and last strand of movements is the Italian Network of Occupied Theatres.[9] Despite inevitably possessing some features that show their organisational continuity with the first two strands, they highlight the way in which the artistic/aesthetical component has come to play. I believe this focus marks a crucial role in the articulation of their requests. In fact, as I will try to briefly sketch in the second section of this chapter, a significant part of the events brought about by this network displays a repertoire of action which includes a massive use of artistic performances and visuals. In the next sections, after a brief outline of the deliberative debate and how its ideals and practices made their way into movements, I will present my case study of Macao, highlighting its peculiar features and why current approaches in social movements are not entirely adequate, and in what ways a (re)think is required regarding mobilised art.

## THE STRUGGLES OF DELIBERATIVE DEMOCRACY

In the context I have briefly outlined, we can interpret the emergence of the deliberative paradigm as being a critique put forth by its theorists regarding the minimal conception of liberal democracy. According to della Porta (2011), deliberative theories developed to cope with the limits of representative democracy. More precisely, they were an attempt to try to include critical citizens within democratic institutions and processes, since a belief was emerging that contemporary democracy had to combine representative and deliberative arenas. The main innovation is that, as against the aggregative model of given preferences posited by the more traditional liberal approach, they advocate a transformation of preferences through a discursive process oriented towards the definition of the common good (della Porta 2011). This deliberation is based on two main tenets: consensus and reason. The first implies that an assembly inspired by deliberative ideals should reach a decision which is approvable by all of its participants, against a majoritarian rule where decisions are legitimised only by vote. A more cautious approach is the one proposed by Chambers (2003, 309) who states that 'consensus need not to be the ultimate aim of deliberation [. . .] legitimacy of outcomes [. . .] ideally characterises deliberation'. Reason is crucial because it represents the ideal medium, under certain conditions, for reaching an intersubjective agreement. Taking up the Habermasian frame (1996) – using reason, emancipation, and rational-critical communication to deliberate and pursue rational interests – deliberation is based on horizontal communicative exchanges, multiple content producers, the possibility of interacting, discussions backed by rational argumentation and a willingness to carefully listen to each other's claims.

The field of deliberative democracy during the last two decades has experienced a golden age involving, in the first instance, a theoretical proliferation and, later, an empirical testing of normative pre-conditions. Attempts to integrate theoretical normative reflection, empirical testing and a subsequent revision of theoretical assumptions have been achieved only recently, as in the case of the latest work of Jürg Steiner (2012), which also includes an interesting opening to storytelling in deliberation, that I will discuss later in this chapter.

A first cleavage in the deliberative debate concerns the different arenas which theorists have in mind. Institutional arenas have been the main focus of Steiner who has mainly dealt with the parliamentary arena (Steiner et al. 2004), and Joerges and Neyer, who were concerned with administrative committees (1997). More inclusive in terms of arenas is the Habermasian proposal elaborated in *Between Facts and Norms* (1996), which entails a double track, with informal deliberation taking place outside institutions, which tries to make its way up through what Habermas defines as the 'hydraulic enclosures' and eventually reaches the inner political system so that public opinion is able to affect institutional deliberation. This process – if redeployed in a less theoretical setting, as in the case of an existing social movement that attempts to produce change at either the symbolic or structural levels – means that the pressure exerted on the 'system' must be adequate to convince the system in turn. However, if one is to take seriously the claim that alternative movements can become institutions 'by themselves' we then have to question the role the political system has. On a superficial level, the political system is avoided, as it is conceived as an entity that is incapable of understanding and giving adequate recognition to something that exists outside of its scope. However, as this book argues, the existing institutional framework is exploited through its blamed inefficiencies and inadequacies precisely to allow for the justification of a new setting to emerge. In order for something new to exist, a claim on the uselessness of the past has to be made (Groys 2014b).

More open to informal deliberation is Dryzek's position. Dryzek (2000) posits that social movements are key actors for the creation of deliberative spaces, even if, in his view, the effect of such informal deliberation is to constitute a critical watch upon institutions rather than productive publics. This latter view is also shared by Mainsbridge (1996) who holds that informal arenas, such as social movements, are conceptualised as enclaves whose most prominent feature should be their distance from institutional power. For our purposes, an interesting analysis of the deliberative approach comes from the work of Iris Young. Young (2003) identified a gap in the approach's rationalistic assumptions, to the extent that she believed that discourse, in a wider understanding, should not exclude other languages or codes of expression; in Young's own words, 'processes engaged and responsible democratic participation include street demonstrations and sit-ins, musical works and cartoons, as much as parliamentary speeches, and letters to the editor' (2003, 119). Such an analysis, although relevant for my perspective – giving an account of the relevance of art for mobilisation and the formation of political cultures – is inadequate, since it is still biased by a progressive paternalistic approach that tries to reassign dignity to popular ways of expressing dissent. A similar attempt in this direction has been made by Kenneth Tucker (2010). It is my belief, however, that beyond the praiseworthy endeavour to recognise such popular repertoires, Young and Tucker fail to capture the constitutive role that art plays in the forging of horizons and possibilities of action, and not just in the last moment of perceivable expression.

Relevant is also the second cleavage in the deliberative debate: that is, the one which concerns the polarity between rational argumentation and a more encompassing view which include practices such as storytelling, humour and narratives in general. For the reconstruction of this debate, we draw upon the excellent analysis made by Steiner (2012) in his latest work. While Steiner's personal position is midway between rational purism – in favour of rational aesthetics, devoid of mercurial human expression – and openness to emotional and personal narratives, a balance between them has to be found according to the context (e.g. a plenary or conference session vs. private meetings). Steiner presents advocates of both sides. On the side of openness we can cite Dryzek (2009, 1181), according to whom 'deliberation can be open to a variety of forms of communication, such as rhetoric, testimony (the telling of stories), and humour. Real-world political communication generally mixes these different forms, and those that do not involve argument can be effective in inducing reflection.'

An opposite view is held by Habermas (cited in Basu 1999, 398) who thinks that 'jokes, fictional representations, irony, games, and so on, rest on intentionally using categorical confusions'. Habermas's position is well known and, on this specific aspect, has been criticised for being blind to how affects are constitutively linked to reasons. Susan Krause, inspired by Hume, affirms that 'deliberation [. . .] is not devoid of intellect, but it involves more than merely intellect. The process of practical reasoning is a holistic one, in which cognition and affect are deeply entwined' (2008, 103); for this reason, she criticises Habermas for not being able to acknowledge how affects and passions are inevitably present in his own concept of rationality. At any rate, this interesting opening made by Steiner and many other scholars regarding the necessity of including different discursive components is surely a positive contribution to the degree that it will help us design more encompassing deliberative practices in institutional settings. Far from being overcome or solved, the dualism of emotion and reason is an archetypical feature of Western culture and a significant contribution in this regard was also recently made within the social movements debate (Goodwin et al. 2001). I will consider this more thoroughly in the next paragraph, where I will stress to what extent this dualism can be useful for the understanding of the Italian artistic mobilisation.

Opening now the scope of our reflection to a wider political-philosophical horizon we can identify a third cleavage (in fact, a clash) between the deliberative paradigm and the agonistic perspective. Pivotal in this regard is the contribution of Chantal Mouffe (1999) whose main point is arguing against the passion for consensus that is so widespread in the deliberative approach. In her account, we should acknowledge that any consensus exists only as the temporary result of a provisional hegemony – understood as a stabilised form of power, which always entails a certain degree of exclusion. For Mouffe, the Habermasian idea that power can be dissolved[10] through a rational debate, and that legitimation might be based on pure rationality, is an illusion which could eventually endanger democratic institutions themselves. For Mouffe, the main aim of any democratic procedure, given an ontological pluralism of values which cannot be reconciled in any consensus-oriented deliberative setting, is to achieve a peculiar form of recognition. A recognition of the other not as a radical other, an antagonist/enemy to be destroyed, but as an adversary – someone whose ideas we fight even while we never question her right to defend those ideas. From this point of view, conceiving the other as a legitimate opponent is the way to achieve what Mouffe defines as the ultimate aim of democratic politics: transforming antagonism into agonism. Such a process requires that passions, in the various forms they take, must find a way to be expressed in relation to issues.

So far, we have concentrated on the clashes within the deliberative literature, and between this perspective and other philosophical conceptions of democracy. Now we propose instead a *paradoxical* continuity that is traceable between the deliberative trend in normative theory and its adoption among social movements over the last two decades. This is a paradox because of the apparent contradiction between the (stereo)typical a(nta)gonistic posture of movements and the orientation towards consensus which seems to be sought within the movements and in negotiations with institutional actors. I believe it is important to investigate this paradoxical link from the perspective of the effects of social science research on society. In other words, the public role of social science research. A sociological starting point for this discussion is the Heideggerian concept of the *hermeneutic circle*, which can be conceived as 'a movement of reciprocal tuning which is produced in the comprehensive investigation between subject and object' (Sparti 2002, 154; my translation from the original Italian). Anthony Giddens (1987) reworks the concept when he posits that social sciences, rather, show a double hermeneutic: that is, they are internal to its subject matter – the study of society – for it always affects or even transforms it by conscious attempts. Moreover, taking up Jeffrey Alexander's thought we can consider how material causes alone 'Without being mediated by cultural representations [. . .] would not have [an] effect' (2011, ix). My attempt here is to include the intellectual production of scholars, a production that not only provides resources to social movements in regard to updating their organisational models but also shapes their understanding of their own cultural activity. The paradox, as I will try to show better in subsequent paragraphs, can be unmasked and shown to be a fake paradox if we orient our gaze towards practices – to the things movements do.

Starting from the genealogical reconstruction proposed by della Porta (2005, 340) we can see how 'movements' activists have adopted and adapted some of the values and norms elaborated within deliberative theories of democracy'. Activists' discussions have sought alternative models of democracy to the elitist, liberal and representative models diffused in contemporary Western democracies. Deliberation shifted also from social movement organisation in the 1960s based on direct democracy and stressing participation. A famous criticism of such a model was proposed by Jo Freeman (1970), by her 'tyranny of structurelessness' concept which reflected the difficulty of implementing principles which stressed participation and the intensity of preferences (i.e. for sets of ideas). The relevant point here is that in the implementation of deliberative values movements gradually lose the communitarian side that emphasises direct action, self-organisation and autonomy. Although these values are still relatively present in many of the 244 movements that are part of the Global Justice Movement surveyed in Donatella della Porta's research (2009) they tend to vanish in more recent organisations and in transnational social movements, in favour of a tendency towards consensus-oriented deliberations.

Another cause of the shift, in addition to the 'scholars' effect' and the deliberations mentioned above, concerns the structural conditions that social movements faced after certain key events. Growing attention has lately been paid to the transformative effects of police repression and political violence, more generally, on the praxis/application of movements. In this sense, we could hypothesise one of the key roles of the riots that took place during the G8 meeting in Genoa 2001 and around 9/11 in the United States. The work of Starr (Starr et al. 2011), for example, makes clear that the first effect of repression is to divert an organisation away from its activist programme and instead commit resources to self-defence. For example, 'one organization that was illegally searched spent more than 1,500 hours of volunteer time dealing with the fallout for its membership and its relations with other organizations' (Starr et al. 2011, 109). Another effect is the replacement of a movement's open culture with a security culture that undermines the movement's politics and practices.

The material and theoretical combination of these three factors has produced what we can define as a *deliberative turn* within the movements. My aim here is not to overstate the relevance of the scholarly debate in this process of change. In fact, as I will try to argue in the next section, the progressive posture embodied in much deliberative theory and the functionalist approach is still very present in the social movements' debate and have led, in my opinion, to a difficulty in capturing the difference brought about by emergent artistically inspired movements. Such difference stems from the fact that, traditionally, these academic debates have neither focused on movements whose constituency was mainly comprised of artists or creatives nor viewed creative repertoires of action as instruments for the mobilisation of non-professionally trained creatives rather than a field itself in which these activists were struggling. Furthermore, as my contribution in this chapter is a theoretical one, my next task will be to highlight such a gap in the social movements debate. A division that derives partially from (a) the relative innovations introduced by Macao as well as other movements by artists/art workers who produce an inter-textual discourse – starting from artistic sensibility through to performative media – and, more generally, by the Italian Network of Occupied Theatres which partially shares some of Macao's organisational features; and (b) the modernist 'echo' still present in social movements studies, as highlighted by Lance Bennett.

The next section will briefly outline the history of Macao and will propose a few examples of how I believe art is playing a constitutive role in the mobilisation. It will also offer a chance to question some of the assumptions of social movements studies.

## MAKING SENSE OF MACAO

To readdress the provisional typology of social movements, from what I have briefly outlined in the introduction, we can now see that what is lacking in the first two experiences – Global Justice Movement and the 'Springs' of 2011 – is an effort to imagine new ways to radically engage with the contradictions of the present. The idea that art can play a role in this task, as it has in the past,[11] is what has driven my interest in what I consider the third strand of movements. This last strand can be traced back to 1 May 2001, when three activist groups initiated the Mayday Parade in Milan: a group of self-organised casual workers, the Chainworkers Crew (workers employed by chain stores), activists belonging to a former Milanese squatted social centre named Bulk, and the local section of the *Confederazione Unitaria di Base*, a radical trade union. During the following years, the core of this movement called for the involvement of more and more activist groups leading to the parade's exponential growth, and to the establishment of a European network against precarious and atypical forms of employment. The early stages of this strand of movements do not present significant differences to more traditional social movements in organisational terms – rather, it is the subject, the atypical jobs and their social and economic questions that begin to be present on the public agenda.

According to Alice Mattoni (2012), most of the mobilisation against precarity occurred during 2004–2005. Two mobilisations are particularly notable as they constitute the beginning of that network of movements of occupied art spaces and theatres in which I am interested, and that will be presented in greater detail later. The first is the 'Reddito per tutt' actions, which saw the birth of the icon of San Precario, an imaginary saint who directs miracles in favour of the less lucky. Artistic performances set up by the Chainworkers Crew spread in the north of Italy and these performances were finally established as a network of social movements, *Grande Alleanza Precaria*. The second mobilisation is the *Serpica Naro* fashion show. The name *Serpica Naro*, an anagram of San Precario, refers to a fake Anglo-Japanese fashion designer that the Chainworkers Crew invented as the face for a real fashion show during the Milan Fashion Week at the end of February 2005. In one sense, the show was a media hoax. In another sense, the fashion show was an unconventional political action linked to the guerrilla communication tradition. Activists mobilised precarious workers employed in the fashion sector to speak about precarity in general and to present a self-produced fashion collection at the Mecca of the global fashion system.

These two cases, embedded in a wider movement, in temporal and spatial terms, began to raise awareness about precarious work conditions and the existence of creative art and knowledge workers. In fact, since 2007 Italy has witnessed a number of artistic occupations, beginning with the *S.a.L.E. Docks*, an independent space for visual arts and experimental theatre born in Venice (thanks to a group of activists who had come from the *Centri Sociali*, self-managed social centres, and from autonomous social movements) with the aim of reversing those processes that privatise the art commons. Since 2011, six more spaces and theatres were occupied throughout Italy, establishing a tight network of movements whose aims exceed the improvement of their own category of art workers and take explicitly into account such issues as citizenship, urban planning, and cultural policy, at the sectorial, local/municipal, and national/international level.

At first glance, it appears to me to be interesting to investigate how a community of openly engaged artists (and sympathisers) deals with such issues – how art influences their capacity to aspire to, and to imagine, spaces for new forms of production and citizenship. This is why I selected Macao, the Milanese 'node' of the network, as a case study. In regard to some of its features, Macao is different from new social movements because, in Macao, art is not just an instrumental tool produced by external or peripheral subjects to the social movement. Furthermore, Macao is not interested in disrupting pre-existing identities, nor do they aim to achieve a recognition of their new identity of art workers by institutions. They are aware (as emerged during a workshop held in early December 2012)[12] of the structural contradictions of their position in the productive system, and the consequently ambivalent nature and extent of their agency. This is why such a case study uncovers issues that are central to my sociological interest. Understanding if, and how, art – a central inspiration for the theoretical and action planning of the movement – can substantially contribute to the prefiguration, and, in the last instance, creation, of radically different public spaces: spaces for citizenship, of course, but spaces which try to go beyond its traditionally acknowledged role within a democracy (Balibar 2011). In other terms, it is about putting to work the material, imaginative and positional excess (Rancière 2007) activists embody in order to transfigure and reconfigure spaces.

Macao became popular in May 2012 because of its occupation of a privately owned skyscraper, Galfa Tower, situated in the former business district of the city. The occupied space functionally served to establish a centre for arts, culture and research, and it symbolically caused a debate about a mass of unused spaces in Milan and, more generally, the role of art and culture in contemporary Italian society that is dominated by radically different interests and priorities. In terms of chronology, Macao is the last movement to join the wave of artistic occupations in Italy (see fig. 1.1). The first of which was the *S.a.L.E. Docks* in Venice, which, as has been said, was established in 2007. The actual and more consistent wave started in April 2011, when art workers occupied the Nuovo Cinema Palazzo in San Lorenzo, a popular neighbourhood in Rome that was being subjected to a process of gentrification. The Palazzo, then being used as a social and cultural space, was about to be turned into a Bingo Hall. One month later, again in Rome, a similar spark led artists to occupy the Valle Theatre. They occupied the theatre because

> the Teatro Valle, a place that is of historical importance for Rome and for the country [was at risk of] [. . .] being awarded to private individuals who [would] betray the nature of a space dedicated to the contemporary theatre scene with an international scope.[13]

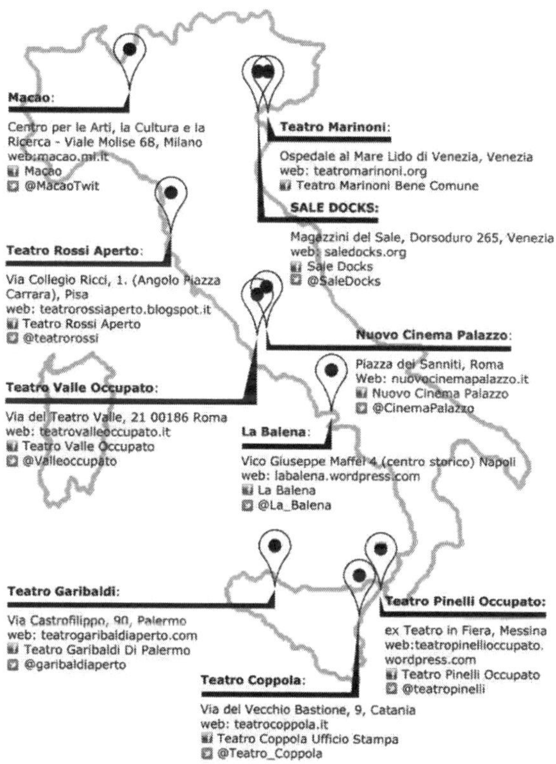


**Figure 1.1 Map of Occupied Theatres in Italy**. *Source*: Silvia Jop.

Occupations continued in Catania (December 2011), Naples (March 2012), Palermo (April 2012), and finally Milan (May 2012).

However, the roots of Macao go back to July 2011, when some of its future members joined the founding meeting of *Lavoratori dell'Arte* (LdA, art workers), a group of artists, critics, curators, journalists and activists who believed that 'art and culture should be a common good and that it is necessary to free them from the political interference which governs their production and determines the precariousness of artists',[14] and 'who verge their specificity and their languages within the common fight to precariousness which, although in different forms, is the hallmark of our times' (Ciccarelli and Allegri 2011, 21). In the following months, the members of LdA (most of whom would later merge into Macao) established links with an emerging network of occupied art spaces and, in December, they took part in their first public demonstration, occupying the Contemporary Art Museum of Milan (PAC). At the end of January, after a meeting, the LdA realised that they needed to commence a 'strongly operative' phase. The end of this phase, after a number of meetings, led to the first occupation of Galfa Tower on 5 May (and ended on 15 May), the second occupation of *Palazzo Citterio* (19–22 May) and the final occupation of *Ex Borsa del Macello*, on 17 June (ongoing).

Macao's activities are now proceeding in two main directions. The first direction, more internal and attended by regulars, takes the form of weekly general assemblies that are open to virtually everyone, and thematic roundtables that involve at least weekly meetings on subjects such as self-building, gardening, communication, workshops, city common goods, laboratories, economy/fundraising, theory and action, video, sound, and hacking. The second direction is Macao's artistic, cultural and entertainment programme, which is directed to a wider audience and to sympathisers (hosting live music, theatre performances, art installations, open and free workshops, a dance hall, a bar service, etc.). In Macao, we trace the presence of typical movement features, such as the use of digital social platforms as tools to organise internally and also to foster the inter-movement network; the use of deliberative procedures to manage long and complex assemblies. The general assembly is held every Tuesday night and gathers about fifty individuals, most of whom take their turn to speak more than once, for an average total duration of four to five hours. The instrumental use of artistic visuals to attract attention: viral mash-up videos[15] and AdBusting[16] procedures which are especially concentrated in the preoccupation moments and the first weeks of occupation, and are spread all over social channels and attract mainstream media attention, and thus mobilise a wider public. This is to say that, of course, we cannot speak of an entirely, radically new approach in regard to every single aspect. However, I think that the interesting logic of the underlying role of art can be grasped if we actively avoid the temptation to reduce the richness embodied in cultural and artistic forms to a simple calculus. In this regard, we should consider what Craig Calhoun talked about when criticising the attempt made by prominent social movements theorists – the need to bring back emotions to the field (Calhoun 2002, 49):

> Most contributors to this volume have tacitly situated their attempts to bring emotions back in as either a challenge or an amendment to the reigning conventional wisdoms of political process theory, resource mobilization, and rational choice. Of course, approaches are not identical, but what they share in common is a more or less instrumental approach to questions of collective action. Instrumental thinking is dominant in the field because of the specific post-1960s struggles that have defined it, but it exists and has the intellectual power it has because of a much longer history linking reason to control (including control over emotions).

Briefly sketching the social movements debate, we can consider how the literature has, on the one hand, underlined that the 'new' social movements intended to address the symbolic codes of society rather than society's material structures (Melucci 1996); on the other hand, scholars have stressed the need to understand the role of emotions in mobilisations, neglected for decades and implicit in many concepts deployed also by more rationalist approaches to social movements (Goodwin et al. 2001). These points of view might well be relevant in research into artists' mobilisation to the extent that the symbolic is the field where art is mostly – although not exclusively – played out, and emotions are the source and the outcome of art performances and aesthetic experiences. Nonetheless, concerning my own particular aims, these points of view are of limited use since they do not take into account art as a field and as a set of visual and performative practices, and as bearers of a public and political function. Art in social movements studies is often understood as a strategic tool that is used in the mobilising or the recruitment process, mainly in the popular and carnivalesque forms it might take in public demonstrations and parades (Tucker 2012), and not as the producer of the field itself and as a contributor to the establishment of a political culture. Considering the peculiar nature of a mobilisation of artists/art workers brought about also by artistic means, as is the case in Macao, my standpoint is that art should be understood in a much more encompassing way.

More recently, the uprisings in North Africa (the Arab Spring), Spain (Indignados) and the United States (Occupy Wall Street, which later spread globally) brought to the fore a debate about the role of digital social platforms in the organisation, recruitment and life of such movements. Bennett and Segerberg (2012), considering the limits of classical approaches to make sense of these emerging phenomena, proposed a typology which differentiates between more traditional movements based on a *collective* logic and an emerging logic that they define as *connective*. The difference is built on the role of formal organisations (unions, advocacy groups, etc.) within the movements: strong in the 'old' movements and marginal or inexistent in the new, large-scale digitally networked mobilisations. In the latter case, digital media are the organising agents whose key role allows individualised actors – bearers of self-motivated personal action frames – to join in more readily, since the costs of cooperation are lowered thanks to the digital communication networks, and therefore the free-riding dogma postulated by Olson (1965) – the difficulty of collecting union dues, for example – is overcome. The organisational shift granted by ubiquitous media, according to Bimber (2005), is even deemed to be responsible for recasting the public/private boundary – requiring a new theoretical understanding of the public and/or the common good. Obviously, the adoption of Information and Communication Technologies is not a unique feature of the most recent mobilisations – Global Justice Movements have adopted them since the late 1990s. The prominent difference is that when digital media are introduced in collective-logic-driven movements they 'do not change the core dynamics of action', while when introduced in connective-logic movements 'they do' (Bennett and Segerberg 2012, 739).[17]

Although they acknowledge the existence of hybrid complex forms where both logics cohabit, the question for Bennett and Segerberg is a matter of definition, and essentially a dualistic one, in which we recognise a typical 'Baumanian' individualised actor whose most prominent activity is to generically 'share content' online. Notwithstanding their criticisms of the contemporary field of social movements, where they still find echoes of a modernist logic that comes out in 'assumptions about the importance of particular forms of organisational coordination and identity in the attention given to organizations, resources, leaders, coalitions [. . .]' (Bennett and Segerberg 2012, 750) their connective/collective dichotomy is still centred around an organisational paradigm to the extent that it envisages a new organisational pattern based on a techno-deterministic interpretation of social digital platforms. In addition to this main criticism I would like to underline how, from my point of view, this perspective fails to grasp what is really happening, to the extent that it ignores the content shared – the *things* which, in Latourian terms, fill the hybrid spaces (urban, local, digital spaces at the same time) of these movements. The attention by movements dedicated to identity, emotions, social networks, political process and opportunity structures is proof of the rejection, most likely only formal, of the core assumptions of resource mobilisation theory. Resource mobilisation involves a pooling of resources: physical resources, such as money or facilities, and non-physical resources, such as the solidarities, cultural commitments, and networks of groups. To reduce free riding, organisers can create selective and/or collective incentives to encourage people to participate.

## (RE)THINKING ART IN MOBILISATION

The relationship between art and mobilisation is multiple and reveals a high level of complexity. Following the connections between the fields of art and mobilisation (Balasinski and Mathieu 2006), we can find at least four ways in which art and mobilisation intersect. In the first place, there is the *engaged artist*, whose talent takes an artistic shape to serve a cause that she feels worthy. Second, there are *collective struggles*, which the art world might term the *enjeux* – to use a French word that is often used by Touraine (literally 'what is at stake'). Such struggles illustrate the stances adopted by representatives of cultural associations or artistic collectives. Another way in which art and mobilisation coalesce is in cases where contentious messages are delivered through artistic pieces.

Although connections among the realms of art and mobilisation are multiple, few studies, especially within the field of social movement studies, have tackled the issue in any detail, with the exception of some isolated examples. Two studies are particularly relevant. The first is that of Ron Eyerman and Andrew Jamison (1998) which analyses the influence of musical traditions on social movements via the relevance of American folk music in the protest wave of the 1960s. Second, the work of T. V. Reed (2005) which, studying the cultural expressions of several North American movements (from the Black Power Movement to the no-global wave), deals with the context of production, the contentious and aesthetic message of these movements, and the effects of their diffusion on society.

This relative lack of interest is even more striking if we consider the overlappings and borrowings that exist or have taken place between the field of art and that of political mobilisation. In the first place, a shared lexicon seems to guide both fields if we think about words as movement and avant-garde (experimental), about both being used in art and in the social and political world to describe collective endeavours willing to establish a new aesthetic or political order. The connections, however, go deeper, if we consider how Howard Becker, in his classical work *Art Worlds* (1984), draws on the resource mobilisation paradigm and uses the notion of 'repertoire of action' – a movements' protest-related tools and actions – which was initially created by Charles Tilly (1986) who, in turn, was inspired by theatre and jazz for the creation of the concept. More recently, James Jasper (2001), who has been culturally oriented in his approach to social movements research, proposed that protest is itself an art, in an attempt to give fuller relevance to the creativity that exists in the actions of social movements. Another relevant overlapping is found in the work of Boltanski and Chiappello (2005), and in their distinction between an artistic critique and a social critique. In a way that is somewhat reminiscent of the *vexata quaestio* (vexed question) between new and old social movements. In Lazzarato's (2007) interpretation, the two different kinds of critique are often developed and embodied by different groups and are incompatible. Furthermore, the artistic critique, which is embodied by highly skilled cultural workers, appears for Boltanski and Chiappello (2000) to be:

> Not in itself necessary to effectively challenge capitalism, a fact demonstrated by the earlier successes of the workers' movement without the support of the artistic critique. From this point of view, May '68 was exceptional. (p. 2)

As we will see in the conclusion, one of the most important aspects of my research is that artists are a crucial component in attempts to challenge capitalism; especially if we consider the increasingly immaterial features that capitalism has assumed in the last three decades. If we combine this insight with an appreciation of the cultural trends in social movement theory we can see that the peculiar relevance of artists in political mobilisation is due to the increasingly symbolic nature of struggles, even the most material ones. Alberto Melucci's work (1996) has insisted precisely on this point and has also tried to unify the different traditions in social movements studies. And it is precisely artists, with their ability not only to decode the complex social and political reality but also to code and produce symbols and signs, who are among the most relevant figures in struggles. In fact, in every social movement that emphasises meaning-making processes (Snow 2001), those social actors that possess a particular form of know-how in terms of production of meaning and manipulation of symbols – that is, artists – come to play a fundamental role.

However, third, to better frame the issue of art in mobilisation we need to orient our sights so as to capture the deeper relevance of art in collective processes. Following Eyerman (2006) we can think of art as an 'imaginative space from which to view the world and from there to represent it' (p. 18). This space is not situated in a sociological void, is not automatically granted an autonomy but is a 'space within the space, a place to view the surrounding world from, yet not untouched by it' (Eyerman and McCormick 2006, 7). As we will see in the following chapters, Macao's activists, in their multiple connections – being artists, workers, and citizens – question even more deeply the idea that being an artist, living like an artist and working like an artist, results in an idyllic and pacified condition.[18] The creativity assigned to art is central to the theoretical elaboration of Eyerman and is connected to his previous work (1998) in which he envisages art as *cognitive praxis,* that is 'a form of social activity through which new kinds of social identities and practices emerge' (Eyerman 2006, 19). From this point of view, art is a social activity and its fundamental mechanic does not differ substantially from other realms of social life. In order to assess art's relevance to mobilisation it is thus important to make clear the context in which its meanings are produced, negotiated and eventually stabilised. To do this, the essential components of a meaningful sociology of the arts, according to Eyerman (2006), are 'a focus on the artwork and the artist while placing both against a complex historical background that includes artist's biography, the history of art, and the current social situation' (p. 26).

Problems arise when the movements to be scrutinised are those, like Macao and the network it is a part of, which are created by artists whose critique inhibits their ability or willingness to create artworks as they are commonly understood in the art world. By artwork, I do not solely refer to pieces with a representational element (painting, sculpture), but also to those abstract and immaterial ideas that are embodied in performances and in the social becoming of art. I mean that to grasp Macao's artistic position we must think of it as a critique of the process of the institutionalisation of social art by the art world and by curators (Bourriaud 2002). This places Macao's artistic production and posture in an unusual position: affirming a social critique through artistic means, refusing the commonly accepted rules that prevail in their own field. This is the reason why, when I was asked during my research about the art in Macao, I tended to answer, somewhat puzzled, that there was little or no art as it is usually understood. This is probably due to the fact that art changes constantly – that art is essentially a mobile frontier. Art and mobilisation, as the formulation itself suggests, appear to be weakly linked: they need a connector. After posing the main research question that inspired this work (how does art change social movements?) I came to realise that there is no direct link between the two and that the connections had to be established in a grounded and contextualised way. Therefore, it is only through a deep and long process of ethnographic research that I have been able to identify the three main areas in which a new kind of art has been changing the processes of social change. The three key dimensions I have identified are action, relation and production.

Concerning the first dimension, my aim has been to analyse the way in which the artists of Macao deploy their political action. By investigating the origins of such action, and the symbolic production related to it, I propose the notion of 'eventful logic' as a new pragmatic concept through which the strategies and the logics of collective action through social media can be satisfactorily explained.

In regard to the second dimension, focusing on the relations and organisation of the movement, I have tried to capture the peculiar mechanics that Macao artists have deployed in order to cope with the functional and political imperatives that confront every movement. What is relevant is how, in their response to such challenges, artists deploy their imaginative excess in a number of different ways so as to create an unstable organisation that is capable of remaining true to life while ensuring efficiency.

In regard to the third and final dimension, I explore the dimension of cultural production in relation to the fact that the Macao artists exist in an urban setting that is guided by a neoliberal form of governance. I highlight how the political mobilisation of Macao not only seeks to compensate for the inefficiencies of the Italian welfare state, but it is also an area in which the radical imagination of the artists-activists of Macao is used to negotiate a position of power with the Municipality.

All of these dimensions are taken into account in my research, as I seek to go beyond an understanding of 'art and social movements' as solely referring to the dimension of protest. In taking this broader perspective, I consider the mobilisation of the artists of Macao as an extremely complex case study through which I hope to shed some light on the current reconfiguration of the relationship between art and criticism. I conclude this chapter with a quotation that I think is extremely relevant in regard to assessing what is at stake in this process of reconfiguration. This is a piece of writing that I came across once I was already engaged in the field, which attests to the extremely recent flourishing of literature on this particular interstitial area. The quotation is from Boris Groys (2014a, 1):

> Current discussions about art are very much centred on the question of art activism – that is, on the ability of art to function as an arena and medium for political protest and social activism. The phenomenon of art activism is central to our time because it is a new phenomenon – quite different from the phenomenon of critical art that became familiar to us during recent decades. Art activists do not want to merely criticise the art system or the general political and social conditions under which this system functions. Rather, they want to change these conditions by means of art – not so much inside the art system but outside it, in reality itself. [. . .] Art activists do want to be useful, to change the world, to make the world a better place – but at the same time, they do not want to cease being artists.

# *Chapter 2*

# Behind-the-Scenes

## *An Ethnography of Artists*

### BACKSTAGE

The first day I visited Macao, in May 2012, the Galfa Tower (a skyscraper) had recently been occupied and I was surprised that I had never noticed that thirty-three-storey building which sat right next to the Pirelli Building, one of Milan's most iconic skyscrapers. I happened to be there with a close friend. Visiting Macao was a way to explore something new that had recently happened in Milan. I was still in the first year of my doctoral programme which involved sitting assessments on research techniques and trying to figure out a suitable research case study.

My master's thesis dealt extensively with public sphere theory (how public opinion becomes political action): I had investigated Italian political blogs to evaluate their democratic potential. Through the works of Jürgen Habermas on public sphere theory, I had also approached literature that revealed the limits of thinking of democratic theory only in rational and discursive, or digressive, terms. Following the inspiring ideas contained in *After Habermas* curated by Nick Crossley (2004) on fresh debates about the public sphere, I was struck by the essay of Michael Gardiner which proposed a juxtaposition between Mikhail Bakhtin and Jürgen Habermas. Gardiner suggested a critique that developed, exactly, the embryonic interest I had formed by the end of my master's thesis: exploring what happens when elements that exceed linguistic limits break into the public sphere. Gardner provides the example of carnivalesque entertainers in the early modern period (1500–1800), where 'existing social hierarchies were often questioned and subverted through carnivalesque strategies of remarkable variety and invention, including the use of parodic and satirical language, grotesque humour, and symbolic degradations and inversions' (2004, 38–39).

Looking at Bakhtin's theory, Gardiner could illuminate the shortcomings of the Habermasian approach:

> Habermas fails to grasp adequately the significance of the embodied, situational and dialogical elements of everyday human life, mainly because his desire to supersede the constraints of a 'subject-centred reason' leads him to embrace an account of intersubjectivity that remains overly abstract and formalistic. In many respects, Habermas is an archetypally modernist thinker, one who strives to achieve a high degree of rational 'purity' and conceptual order. (Gardiner 2004, 29)

Departing from such understanding, it became clearer to me that the intellectual posture embodied in the theory of the public sphere was a tool that, as a result of Habermas's orderliness, lacked sociological realism – as Nancy Fraser voiced in her famous critique (Fraser 1990, 1992). As my theoretical interests changed, professional and political experiences also contributed to the reorientation of my sociological focus. A key experience in this journey was my involvement in the organisation of a theatre festival in Siena, in 2011. At this time I saw Emanuele, one of the founders of Macao, rehearse a choreography that Balletto Civile – a theatre company Emanuele co-founded – had to perform at short notice because a theatre group had made a last-minute cancellation. The festival was part of a broader European project coordinated by friends and colleagues in Siena and it explored the issue of the creolisation in culture; namely, the processes through which neighbouring cultures integrate to create a new one. I only realised one year later that Emanuele, whom I had seen dancing but had never spoken to, was part of the group that started Macao in June 2012. I can still remember the feeling of rapture I had watching the two dancers holding hands, facing each other and spinning around a trampoline with the vaults of the medieval frescoed hall of Santa Maria della Scala framing them.

During the spring of 2011, other colleagues from the University of Siena became part of a movement against a law privatising water services in Italy; campaigning for a referendum on public water. As I took part in their roundtables and debates, I familiarised myself with the emerging Commons paradigm (Mattei 2011). Initially used as a way to frame the idea of a common good par excellence, such as water, the Commons paradigm later became the central theme for occupied theatres which extended the notion of self-organised social systems to culture and knowledge being accessible to everyone (Hess and Ostrom 2011). At the same time, theoretical discussions developed around the meetings of *Lavoro Culturale* (the Cultural Work), a series of seminars I co-organised in Siena. The blog[1] we set up to publish materials from these seminars later became a wider space for cultural debate; for instance, hosting contributions that covered the first occupation of Teatro Valle in Rome (June 2011) by posting interviews with their protagonists.

It was in this context of political and cultural effervescence that my intellectual and research interests developed and progressed in new directions. Closely following the events of the spring of 2011 was a true inspiration for me to undertake research on the movements that supported the campaign for public water – focusing in particular on their creative and performative elements. As I drew closer to the movement, attending meetings such as the European Social Forum, held in Florence in November 2011, I realised that I was not interested so much in the performances and creative displays usually developed for use in demonstrations and protest actions. I was interested in how artists were reshaping the political field via their engagement in the public sphere. As I eventually came to realise, Macao constituted an excellent vantage point from which to observe the kind of processes I had studied in theoretical form over the previous year.

I believe that for a sociologist, and especially for a qualitative sociologist who adopts an ethnographic framework, it is important to provide an account of the backstage setting of any study. The central purpose of this chapter is to explain my ethnographic perspective, while endeavouring to outline the methodological literature on the fascinating area of autoethnography.

> The term [autoethnography] has a double sense – referring either to the ethnography of one's own group or to autobiographical writing that has ethnographic interest. Thus, either a self- (auto-) ethnography or an autobiographical (auto-) ethnography can be signalled by 'autoethnography'. (Reed-Danahay 1997, 2)

Notwithstanding the fact that it is increasingly difficult to define what is meant by 'an artist', I can confidently define myself as a not-artist as I have been drawn into this world as a researcher via my interest in political social movements. Thus, I am tied to my fieldwork by multiple personal connections, by overlapping domains of work and life, and by my belief that the cultural and artistic mobilisation that commenced in June 2011 is probably one of the most productive and one of the widest mobilisations that Italy has seen, since the turning point of Genoa in 2001. Theory, life, friendships and passions are all equally constitutive of the endeavours of a sociologist, and thus I deem it necessary to account for them publicly. Since research and life adjoin one another in my case I think transparency and accountability are fundamental to secure the validity of the qualitative work I have conducted.

## ONSTAGE: GETTING IN, GETTING ON

Traditionally, two phases define the relation of the ethnographer to the field (Buchanan et al. 1988): 'getting in' and 'getting on'. In this part, I will present the phases that characterised gaining access to Macao.

### Getting In

I started following Macao's activity in the early days of the movement in 2011, but I chose Macao as my ethnographic field of study only months later: during the late summer of 2012. I had decided to make Macao my main field of ethnographic enquiry. During those interstitial months, I had been following them closely on social media, reading their press releases and gathering data about their online activity. After being evicted from occupying the Galfa Tower, from 5 to 15 May, they symbolically occupied other spaces and then eventually moved into the Exchange, a former slaughterhouse, in June. The first time I visited their new home was 6 November 2012. I wanted to see this space that they had occupied in June and restored throughout the summer (see Strong Ties). Box 2.1 presents my first fieldnotes.

#### BOX 2.1. FIELDNOTES: THE EXCHANGE

Tuesday, 6 November. It is around 10.00 pm and the main hall of Macao is almost empty. There are about fifteen people around. Some play chess sitting at a small table, while at a bigger table near the bar the artists that are going to perform later are being served their meal. It is rather cold in here, and no heating seems available. I have read on their website that today's event is part of the *Exp_Nov* series, consecrated to experimental visuals and music. A vintage stop-motion movie is projected on a mega screen in the hall, shortly after I realise it's a collection of short movies by the Canadian director and animator Norman McLaren. As I get a drink at the bar, I have the chance to listen to some conversations. The first barman acknowledges to another customer that drinks are not of the highest quality. Later he would say that he has been living and working in Macao in the last six months, that is, from the beginning. Shortly after I overhear another conversation, another bartender says she is about to move to San Francisco where her boyfriend, who she has not met in the last two and half months, currently lives. Notwithstanding the cold, she is lightly and finely dressed. She gives the impression of taking her role seriously, as in believing that doing professionally a job/task that requires interaction with a public implies conveying a good impression.

> Meanwhile, a musician is conducting his soundcheck producing dissonant sounds. As I sip my drink, I type this sentence on my mobile phone, as I did not want to be seen taking notes in a notebook: 'Art represents for Macao the professional and cultural background of its constituency and, at the same time, the economic backbone of their cultural and artistic offer'. [Later in the evening] I am impressed by how efficient two people are in taking the chairs from another room and orderly distributing them across the room almost automatically. In addition, my attention is attracted by the considerable amount of technical equipment for the show. Where is it coming from? [I decide to visit the rest of the building. I go upstairs, in some rooms there are video installations, and I can have an overview of the space, which appears] beautiful in its liberty-style decadence and harmony.

The second time I visited Macao was in early December 2012 for a weekend-long seminar that addressed artistic and cultural production in the 'social factory' a concept by Tronti (1966) referring to labour becoming decentralised, out with the factory into the broader social sphere: a 'factory without walls'. Macao also presented the results of a self-inquiry conducted over the previous months to investigate Macao's constituency (Macao 2012a). The seminar was titled '69,300 hours', this number representing the amount of time that activists had devoted to Macao in its first six months. The seminar, see figure 2.1, was a chance for me to discover the specificities of the analysis conducted by Macao and the community that Macao connected and gathered, such as academics, practitioners and activists with interests ranging from economics to art and cultural criticism. Concerning my access to the field, this seminar was an important step because it allowed me to understand what kind of approach was most suitable for my research. A friend of mine from Siena was there and he personally knew one of the Macao founders, Emanuele, which facilitated access as during a break my friend introduced me, explaining to him that I was conducting a PhD about the relationship between art and political mobilisation. Perhaps due to that particular moment in time or fatigue, since Emanuele was heavily involved in managing and moderating the seminar, his reply was short but substantial. His message was 'participation is the only way in'. This was not necessarily a bad or a negative reply, but not having the chance to engage in a follow-up discussion resulted in a missed chance for me, and produced some concerns about the possibility of accessing the field: would Macao welcome research within their organisation or be close-minded? From this initial meeting, I decided that the way to access the community was through direct participation and contribution.

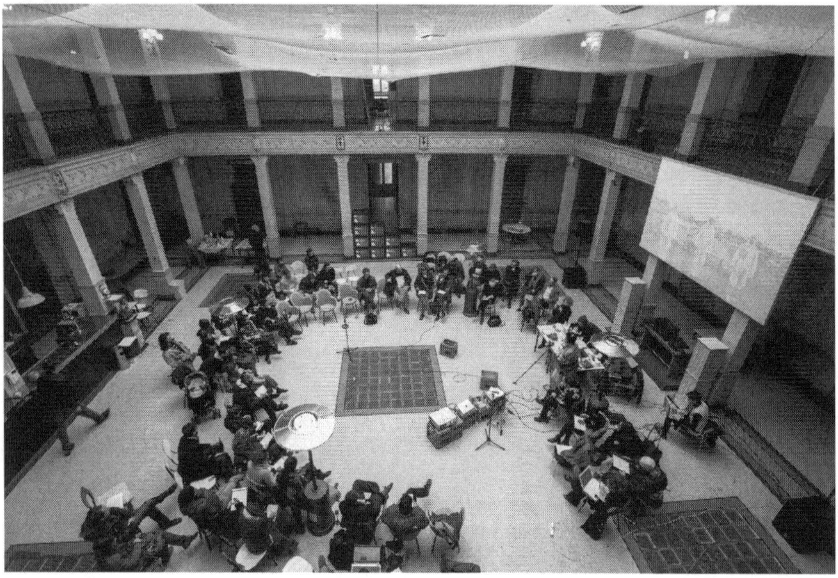

**Figure 2.1 Macao during an Assembly**. *Source*: Luca Chiaudano.

In February 2013, I discussed my field access issues with a PhD colleague. I had been trying to locate 'entrance' points into the organisation through acquaintances and found out that she was in touch with another member of Macao, the treasurer, and agreed to set up a meeting. On another cold Tuesday, I met with Chiara and Rachela, treasurer and member of the 'architecture working group', respectively. We met at 7.00 pm in a small family-run restaurant just in front Macao[2] for me to present my project thoroughly and communicate my intention to undertake an ethnography there. The response was positive and welcoming. From this point onwards, there was a rapid and intense acceleration of research, detailed below.

## GETTING ON

The second phase of accessing the field moved towards a deeper participation in Macao's activities. Inspired by the idea that an engaged implication in the field constitutes a way of contributing to a deeper sociological understanding and to knowledge that is useful to social movements (Mirzoeff 2013), the first step in this phase was to take part in Macao's project relating to the 'publics' an economic analysis of Fuorisalone – an off-event that runs parallel to Milan Design Week – which investigated the working conditions and the redistribution of the value created by the event across the whole supply chain. During the first assembly in early December, while discussing this project and its eventual developments, I decided to contribute actively and proposed integrating digital methods to analyse the work carried out by the thousands of people that tweet and take pictures on Instagram during Fuorisalone. Thus began a deeply interesting journey, which involved the so-called tagging nights in June 2013 where tens of people worked together to code the pictures that I, together with other fellows of the Centre for Digital Ethnography of the University of Milan (CDEUM 2021), had gathered.

However, by becoming a complete participant, the process of 'getting on' risked turning into an ethnographically undesirable piece of work. Considering the range of ethnographic positions that a researcher can embody (Hammersley and Atknison 1995, 104), I realised I had shifted rapidly from being a complete observer to what Hammersley and Atknison define as 'comparative involvement', in which the researcher's subjectivity and her sympathy become a reflexive part of the investigation. I was reminded of this critical issue in the summer of 2013 when Macao was invited to make a presentation of its global activities during a musical and cultural festival in Padua (Sherwood Festival 2021). One of the main ongoing projects at that time was the one in which I was involved and I was asked to take part by giving a short presentation on how I was deploying digital methods in this research. The festival organisers referred to me as 'Alberto from the Centre for Digital Ethnography of Milan', whereas Emanuele promptly rectified, not without a hint of amusement, that it was actually 'Alberto from Macao'. As I will highlight in the final section of this chapter, Emanuele and Macao, in general, are completely aware of the issues and the ambiguities of their positioning in the political field, including my political positioning in the sociological field. This surprising event reinforced the attention I gave to how I was negotiating my position within Macao. From that moment onwards, I realised that, because of the projects I was following or participating in, I risked being over-identified by a part of the constituency of Macao as someone that 'belonged' to a particular faction within the movement. Such a risk of over-identification is somehow embedded in the ethnographic practice itself, to the extent that it relies on key informants. Furthermore, as personal and professional connections tied me to certain activists more than other affinities and friendships developed beyond the research.

In other words, given these social and professional roles within Macao, I risked neglecting other important parts of the fieldwork. To cope with and to try to avoid this risk, I combined the eighteen-month time span I had planned to spend in the field with a reflexive understanding of my position that allowed me to cover the life and projects of Macao more thoroughly over the subsequent months.

## OFFSTAGE: CASE SELECTION AND RESEARCH TECHNIQUES

The question that I often asked myself was if, and to what extent, a comparative analysis could have been beneficial for this research project. The methodological literature regarding social movements rarely considers a single-sited ethnography as a viable solution – two different options is the most widespread technique in recent studies of political mobilisation: also known as the comparative case study or variable-based approach. An influential contribution is della Porta's methods for social movement research. In particular, comparing the two main strategies adopted within the field – that is, a small-N, case-oriented approach and a quantitative variable-based approach – she states:

> Focusing on a small-N, case-oriented comparison usually points at similarities and differences through dense narratives, with a large number of characteristics being taken into account, often together with their interaction within long-lasting processes. (della Porta 2008, 204)

However, I believe that employing this technique, even if discerning for the close examination of selected cases, a comparison would not have allowed me to access the fine cultural bricolage that often exists in movements. Following Melucci (1994), as conflicts promoted by movements 'raise a challenge that recasts the language and cultural codes that organise information' (Melucci 1994, 102), the deepest possible level of depth is required in order to grasp such recasting. In this sense, as highlighted by Combes et al. (2011), there is a certain risk of methodological *routinisation* within research on social movements. Combes argues how the pioneering works of Charles Tilly on the morphology of contentious/collective action, based on longitudinal statistical studies, have inspired a quantitative research tradition that is interested in measuring the geographical or temporal variations of contentious actions. Following Tilly's line of thought, morphology represents the visible structure while the contentious/collective dynamic stresses different subjective positions: those in power, those who are not and those who are challenging political power with adversarial ideas. These groups have conflicting interests, and sometimes this disagreement grows into a coherent social movement that is organised and systematised. Additionally, the longitudinal dimension is deployed to grasp morphological changes in the *longue durée*; that is, how contentious politics changes across decades or centuries (e.g. from the French Revolution to the bourgeois revolutions of the late eighteenth century and working-class struggles in the twentieth century).

Globally, Combes argues, it is the comparative approach in itself that must be questioned. Often, comparability between movements that appear to share similar goals in different countries is taken for granted even if, at closer inspection, we can observe extreme heterogeneity under the same denomination. Furthermore, the multiplication of sites of comparison contributes to a loss of in-depth analysis and in the precision of the data gathered, often dealing with variables whose specificity has been flattened to make them comparable. In this context, according to Combes, the only way to reinject dynamism into the study of social movements is to return to direct ethnographic engagement in the field.

The choice to carry out a single-sited ethnography for this study was also due to Macao's complexity. The activists themselves acknowledged this complexity as they experienced difficulty keeping pace with the movement's constant effervescence. Adhering to Melucci's (1996) guidance once more, I have tried to systematise the complexity embodied in Macao. Contemporary movements are solidarity networks – bearers of powerful cultural meanings; they are also systems of action – complex networks of diverse levels of social action. For such movements collective identity is not a given; it is the outcome of exchanges, negotiations, decisions and conflicts among actors. Additionally, movements are constructed upon several layers. Melucci analytically distinguishes these layers as being processes of mobilisation and organisation, forms and models of leadership and ideologies, and forms of communication from within the action system that constitutes the collective actor. Internally relations with competitors, allies and adversaries exist, and, not least, within the context of a political system that defines the field of opportunities. It is because of such complexity, which characterises Macao and the multiple networks in which it is embedded, that the best way to approach these dimensions was to limit the scope of my research to a single-sited ethnography. In addition, I conducted twenty-four semi-structured interviews that covered the biographic dimensions of the activists and their own views concerning their engagement in Macao. Most interviews were conducted at Macao between November 2013 and January 2014 at the end of the fieldwork. I have anonymised participants by codes numbered from 50 to 70, to 100 (e.g. MI 1, MI 2, MI 3, etc.).

So far, I have adopted the term 'single-sited' when referring to my ethnography. Yet if we consider the overlapping levels of which Macao is itself made, its network, its alliances, the economic flows that affect them, and the urban context, my research can hardly be considered as a true single-sited ethnography. In particular, one domain has proved to be another site of ethnography entirely: the digital realm. Following the reflections that have been expounded in the anthropological field over the last two decades, increasing complexity has resulted in a widespread adoption of multi-sited ethnography.

Cross-cutting old dichotomies such as 'local' and 'global', the 'lifeworld' and the 'system', the 'emergence of multi-sited ethnography are located within new spheres of interdisciplinary work, including media studies, science and technology studies, and cultural studies more broadly' (Marcus 1995, 95). In the interest of dealing with the digital aspects of this study's ethnography, I have adopted a web-based approach – so-called digital ethnography (Caliandro 2015). This method is mainly defined as a series of methods that are natively digital, unlike virtual-ethnography (Hine 2000) whose methodological strategy is developed offline and only then applied to the online environment.

Online implies following social media platforms, Instagram tags and Twitter re-tweets, and the structural flows of information and communication. Digital techniques I have deployed during my research include co-word analysis (considering keywords and the strength of their associations within a document), semantic analysis (identifying contextual clues in the data from words and grammatical structures and their relational meanings) and network analysis (concerning social relations/structures). My work on Macao's digital realm constituted an obvious point of entrance to the fieldwork; in that, it allowed me to familiarise myself with Macao's discursive production in terms of text and in terms of the interactions between the Macao activists and their online publics. Later on, digital ethnography also allowed me to compare and validate my findings via 'traditional' ethnography. A relevant example can be found in figure 2.2, a graphic elaboration of the links established by the Macao Facebook page. Following the 'natives', the actor in this scenario is often the team or the single individual that manages the Facebook page of the group who, with his act of liking another page, establishes a link (an 'edge', in network analysis terminology), while each community, represented by its page, represents a node in the network.

The data used to create this graph was gathered through Netvizz, a Facebook application created by Bernhard Rieder (2013). The dataset consists of 7,000 nodes and more than 60,000 edges, displaying a gathering strategy inspired by a big-data approach. Which basically means gathering large amounts of information. To produce a broad picture during the process of data gathering, I extended the capture process to include not only the links directly established by Macao with other pages but also the links that these other pages directly made to Macao, among themselves and other nodes. As my traditional ethnography approach progressed I hypothesised that Macao's mobilisation was more closely linked to the realm of Milanese cultural production (think tanks, start-ups, blogs and the makers' scene) rather than a network of Milanese social centres.

Digital analysis made it possible to manage an amount of data that would otherwise have been impossible to handle. The nodes visible in the

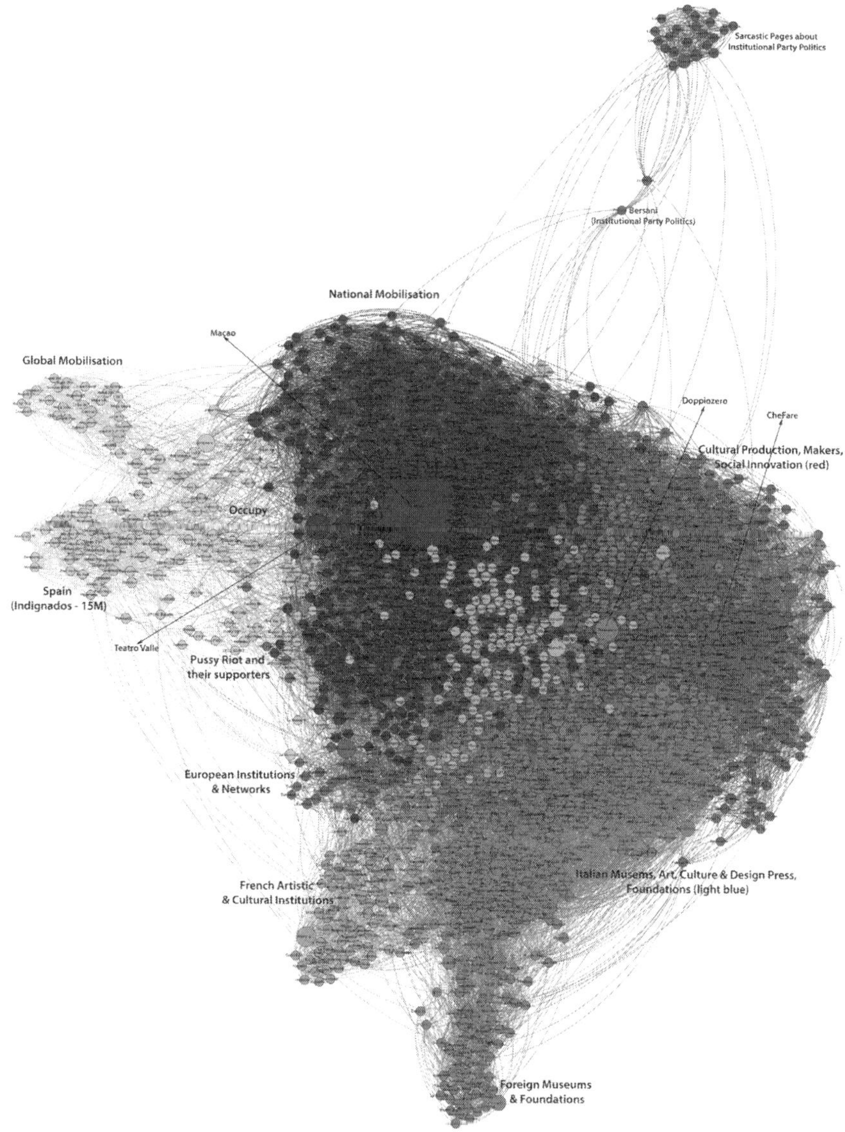


**Figure 2.2 Like-Network of Macao's Facebook Page Visualised in Gephi**. *Source*: Created by author.

map are part of the 'giant component' of the network – only the nodes that are part of the main network cluster. This visualisation of the nodes and their distance from the centre (the Macao node – the biggest node in the network, because it is the node we start from) is the result of two main measurements: centrality and eccentricity. The first indicates how close a node is to the other nodes in an entire network and whether or not the node lies on the shortest path between other nodes, while the second captures the distance between a node and the node that is furthest from it; so a high eccentricity means that the furthest node in the network is a long way away, and a low eccentricity means that the furthest node is quite close. Looking at the graph, for instance, it is not surprising to find that Bersani (former leader of the Democratic Party, which has a centre-left political orientation) is at the top of the graph, and is relatively isolated from the rest of the network.

However, this is not the most relevant insight this kind of data visualisation gave me. To begin with, the connection between Macao and global mobilisation (the yellow cluster on the left) is relatively distant and is mediated by the Teatro Valle, a true hub in terms of digital connections within the Italian Network of Occupied Theatres, but it is also relatively more connected with global social movements (Occupy and Indignados, in particular). Additionally, what we can consider as 'contaminations' within the homogenous cluster reveal Macao's peculiar interests and the degree of development of networks in that direction. On the right side is a blue cluster representing Macao (that broadly includes Italian movements and sympathetic media outlets, for the most part), here we can observe a number of light-yellow nodes that manage to get 'in'. These are mainly pages related to cinematographic projects linked with Macao or, more precisely, with the Video Working Group, which is one of the most active and visible working groups within Macao.

Having said that, the data retrieved from Facebook show more ethnographically interesting links with the light blue cluster (representing an area of culture: including museums and foundations, as well as less established and more informal actors, such as blogs and media outlets that deal with culture, mainly from Spain and Italy) and the red cluster (representing a rather homogenous collection of think tanks, start-ups, maker spaces, etc.). Moreover, the culture cluster groups, at the bottom end, Italian cultural institutions, and bordering the blue-cluster Italian contemporary art institutions. They also include nodes representing the most institutional actors in the cultural field in Spain, and moving towards the top of the graph. The relevant point here is that in this area one node is noticeable for its size (showing a high betweenness centrality): this is Doppiozero, a cultural blog that has been extremely influential in the debate about traditional highbrow culture (poetry, literature) and social and cultural innovations (new social practices). This digital ethnography reveals that Macao has participated in a public call for funding cultural projects promoted by Doppiozero, and thus shows, through the application of digital methods, the network of alliances and affinities of which Macao is a part.

In this kind of scenario, and increasingly in social research, digital methods represent a stand-alone technique that can be used to pursue research in online spaces, or they represent a fundamental component of ethnography, given the inextricable link between online and offline in the life and activities of a movement and its activists.

# Chapter 3

# Art's Own Activism

Artists are at the frontlines of political mobilisation, due to the peculiar social and economic situation that affects them in a direct and an indirect way. They mobilise themselves and try to aggregate fellow citizens around ideas of radical citizenship and self-governance: but they do so in their own peculiar way. This chapter focuses on the occupation of Galfa Tower, the event through which Macao was born, on 5 May 2012, and which contributed to the development of its fundamental lines of existence. The main aim of the current chapter is to investigate what happens when artists' tools are mobilised in physical spaces and digitally mediated environments. A situated and microphysical point of view (or the sociology of everyday life) is useful as it enables me to give an account of the specific role played by art in mobilisation, and to avoid the risk of overlooking the elemental components of action; that is, the actions of an individual arising in a social context. A more thorough consideration of such components can contribute to a deeper understanding of the aesthetic, affective, cultural, political and ethical stances that are responsible for the existence and the shaping of the 'stitching mechanisms' (Bennett et al. 2014) at work in large-scale digitally mediated movements. For example, Bennett et al. (2014, 272) identify Twitter as a key digital, stitching mechanism 'used to coordinate other actors and platforms within the wider protest ecology'. Relating this to Macao, as a result of the organisation's intense reliance on cultural, social and affective dynamics its mobilisation offers a vantage point from which to reassess the assumptions that have guided our understanding of the recent wave of mobilisations in terms of connective action and to update our understanding of the linkages between art and political mobilisation.

The chapter is divided into four main parts. The first tackles the issues that arise when defining what is a somewhat slippery object of analysis (the mobilisation of artists), given the number of concurrent perspectives that can be used to interpret artists and their actions. The second part consists of an ethnographic narration regarding the road paved by Macao activists in the Galfa Tower event. The third part of the chapter complements and contrasts the second, by describing and analysing patterns of social media communication adopted before and during the occupation of the Galfa Tower. The last part proposes 'eventful logic' as a pragmatic concept which can be used to explain the dynamics of the emergent wave of artistic mobilisation.

## A MAGIC HAT IN A DIGITAL WORLD

As previously discussed (in chapter 1), a fundamental task when seeking to understand art *in* mobilisation concerns its framing as a 'productive field'. I mean that, although performances, chants, choreographies, puppets and other creative or artistic performances have been somewhat taken into account in the scholarly literature in at least three different fields (social movement studies, sociology of arts and sociology of culture) the problem is that often (Tucker 2012) these works, although inspiring, reveal a conceptualisation of art in mobilisation which is limited (for my purposes), for two fundamental reasons: objectivation and instrumentalisation.

The first problem lies in arbitrary segmentation when only the perceivable expression of creative acts are being analysed that, by definition, are the product of complex processes.[1] From this point of view, what are to be investigated are mostly the effects of the visible presence of a creative product on its reception context, which is often one of protest. This leads to the second problem. As social movement scholars have explained (della Porta and Diani 2006), protest is one of the many ways in which political mobilisation takes place. Marches, rallies, demonstrations and parades undoubtedly constitute some of the key arenas in which creative performances are publicly staged in an attempt to attain visibility and recognition for the movements and the causes that they advocate. Furthermore, protests have traditionally been organised by social movements or coalitions (Diani 1992), or, according to Bennett and Segerberg (2013) and Castells (2012), by crowds themselves, the most fundamental unit of which is the *activist*.

Accordingly, the main question which scholars – in particular, the few who explicitly deal with art and social movements (Balasinski and Mathieu 2006; Eyerman and Jamison 1998; Reed 2005) – have posed can typically be rephrased as: How are activists using art in mobilisation? In a nutshell, the underlying assumption is that art, performances and creativity can be assimilated into a 'colourful magic hat' out of which activists can draw innovative tactics for a successful protest. Using more formalised language, art and aesthetics constitute a subgroup of a wider repertoire of action that a given social movement is able to activate.[2] Of course, this perspective is still perfectly viable, and what is being questioned here is not the capacity of such a perspective to explain what has happened over the last decades or in contemporary occurrences in which art and protest have been linked instrumentally (or are understood as such). In empirical terms, this is the case when a non-professional artistic activist uses their creativity in protest or co-opts professional artists for the production of protest artefacts.[3] Consider the following words by a Reclaim the Streets activist (Pink & Silver Brigades):

> For me [. . .] the Pink and Silver was tactical frivolity [. . .] so you are using frivolousness [. . .] tactically in a situation where everyone is geared up for confrontation. (Exposito and Vila 2007)[4]

Looking back at the late 1990s, the interviewed activist sees frivolousness as a tactic to be deployed in effective protesting, for example, to draw police attention to herself and to divert it from something going on elsewhere. However, such an approach shows its limits when the only people involved are artists themselves, mobilising on their own.

Art and politics, the politics of aesthetics and the aesthetics of politics, politicised artists and avant-gardes have produced, and have themselves been, widely debated topics in Western thought. Additionally, it is not just in speculation that the two realms have crossed paths. As Mathieu Gregoire (2013) highlights in his recent book, the *Intermittents du Spectacle*, a specific category of French art workers,[5] have engaged for the whole of the last century in a struggle for their rights. From these premises, to conclude that there is nothing new in artists' mobilisations would be equally wrong. In fact, Gregoire's main argument is that, starting from reasons and desires that appear consistent throughout the century, art workers have constructed distinct emancipatory horizons[6] over time. What is revealing is that through these different lenses it is possible to reconstruct the underlying logic of the global social conflict in a given context. To better frame the context which Macao's mobilisation is part of, we now must take into account the prominent role that digital media have come to play.

The diffusion of Information and Communication Technology (ICT) has attracted growing attention within the interdisciplinary field of contentious politics (Tilly and Tarrow 2007). Contributions in this field have stressed if, and to what extent, ICT has reshaped modes and practices of political mobilisation. In particular, along with technological development questions regarding 'whether organizations still have a role in grassroots mobilisation, whether dense face-to-face community networks are still necessary to support collective action, whether identity bonds still need some kind of shared direct experience and/or 'real' interaction to develop' (della Porta and Diani 2006, 132) started to emerge after the 1990s. From the outset, the social movement debate seems to frame the articulation of media and mobilisation by privileging an organisational point of view.

More recently, uprisings in North Africa (the Arab Spring), Spain (Indignados) and the United States (Occupy Wall Street, which then globally spread as a 'protest brand') have renewed the debate on the role of social media in the organisation, recruitment and life of these mobilisations. In this context, Lance Bennett and Alexandra Segerberg (2013) propose a typology that differentiates between movements based on a more traditional collective logic compared to emerging connective logic in which the digital media are the organising agents. In a nutshell, their proposal is to analytically differentiate collective action as well organised and based on central organisations (such as the union, the party, the movement based on class and shared interests); whereas the role of central organisations in connective action is greatly diminished, and social media provide the 'stitching' among very different individuals who do not necessarily share fundamental traits. According to Bennett and Segerberg, this is needed to ensure that digital activists can feel a togetherness in their intents and aims. Dealing with the same wave of mobilisation, Manuel Castells (2012) identifies a fundamental common feature among them: their being inextricably linked to the creation of autonomous communication networks, supported by the internet, and, in particular, by wireless services. This feature separates them from previous experiences, so that they are not just social movements anymore: they are networked social movements.[7]

Within this overarching framework, what I propose is that through the case study of Macao it is possible to shed some light on what is, perceivably, an emerging mobilisation logic: a logic that I define, in an attempt to bridge the contentious fields of politics, digital media research and cultural sociology, as an *eventful logic*.

## STROLLING TO THE SKYSCRAPER

The extract below, written by Macao in September 2014, was enclosed in a press kit to support its first fundraising campaign since its establishment in 2012.[8]

> Macao becomes visible to the city of Milan through the liberation of Galfa Tower – an excellent piece of post-war modern architecture and a symbol of financial speculation within the Milanese territory which was abandoned and 'frozen' for more than a decade in the real estate portfolio of the Ligresti family.

> Working groups, research groups and experimental groups, focusing on the wide-ranging languages of contemporary arts, were born here. Now they operate in the former, and disused, Exchange of the municipal slaughterhouse situated in Viale Molise 68, a perfect example of Liberty in Milan, in a densely populated neighbourhood hosting a number of different cultures, working conditions and incomes. Here practices and reflections are open to contributions from all people, and they mark a radical model of active citizenship that finds its expression in working groups, in assemblies, in the care of the space, in the production of art and culture. These practices and reflections are embodied in Macao's relations with social centres, neighbourhood associations and individual citizens, but also with research and cultural institutions (from museums to universities) to create seminars, projects and co-productions. A free use and diffusion of culture, independent co-production under Creative Commons, the research into and the experimentation with new economies, the sharing of space and equipment and cultural dialogue constitutes just some of the branches of Macao's current research and practices. (Macao 2014; my translation)

This description helps us to understand what Macao now is, and what its main lines of research are. However, we need to take a step backwards and see how Macao has reached this point. Macao, as an idea, was born in a room several months before the occupation of a skyscraper. It was the winter between 2011 and 2012, and the group of five people who were sitting in that room were what was left of a wider group called *Lavoratori dell'Arte* (art workers – LdA in the text hereafter).

This group was formed in the summer of 2011, after some of their members got in touch with the first occupations which started in Rome in June 2011 – Teatro Valle was occupied on 14 June, exactly one day after the historical victory in the referendum on 'water as a common good', against the privatisation of public water. When they returned to Milan, these members started organising assemblies, which started to gather a wider public, including knowledge workers and 'material', or manual, workers who had been laid-off. Already, at this early stage, two elements were visible that helped delineate the ideas of the future founders of Macao: in the first instance, they disagreed with what they deemed was the dominant attitude of those assemblies – precariousness in terms of self-pity, which consisted of an individualist sharing of negative experiences, in terms of jobs and life quality. In the second instance, the LdA felt an urge to take proactive and radical action. But to understand what kind of action they had in mind, it is necessary to take a further step back.

In 2010, the informal group who later founded the LdA realised that they had a common 'disease' in that, as one interviewee shared with me, they were 'incompatible with the visual arts' working system' (MI 2), which they considered to be based on exploitation and devoid of any kind of formal protection for artists vis-à-vis the institutional art system. Their idea in forming the group was, therefore, to develop a set of formalised contracts to protect artists from one that had been created in Germany by a group of artists and lawyers (MI 2). This legal translation effort within the framework of Italian law proved fruitful in theory, but less so in practice. Such contracts have been adopted by no one in the arts sector, showing the Italian art system to be impervious to a change in this direction.[9] This anecdote shows the radically different situation faced by Italian artists compared to their colleagues in France, the *Intermittents.* The field of Italian art workers was fragmented, isolated and without the support of traditional transmission belts, such as unions and parties. It is from this context that a new horizon of emancipation derived. Its defining feature being a shift from a policy-oriented struggle to a more encompassing political struggle to protect and advance artists' rights and interests.[10]

A rupture within LdA took place when the artistic wing of the group – the other wing being mainly curatorial – decided to symbolically occupy, for a day, the contemporary art museum in Milan, *Padiglione d'Arte Contemporanea* (PAC). The museum was hosting an exhibition by Pixar, the American animation giant. The main reason for this rupture lay in the different perspectives regarding what precise form practices of social change should take. In the words of a LdA member, later a founder of Macao (MI 3):

> Radicalism is not a thought, it is first and foremost a practice. If you limit yourself to the level of thought, you are confined within the aestheticization of the struggle [. . .] we had a compelling desire to get rid of the concept of participation and listening. Later on we cared but in that moment we did not.

These ideas resonate with a situationist heritage, an indirect predecessor of this emerging mobilisation,[11] and they are also relevant to assess the development of Macao's mobilisation. After this split, the five remaining art workers 'closed themselves in a room for a month' (MI 2) and, eventually, came up with an idea: to occupy the Galfa Tower. A campaign to anticipate this occupation was carefully planned, involving social media and Milan's urban space. The success of this campaign on digital terms will be evaluated in the following paragraphs. What is important to underline here is the role of detailed planning that was behind the Galfa Tower *event,* alongside the coupling of physical and digital dimensions.

The path that led to the Galfa Tower occupation involved a number of different elements. First, assemblies were called in various social spaces in Milan, which gathered hundreds of people (according to different interview participants such as MI 1, MI 3, MI 5 and MI 9), in March and April 2012.

Second, a video campaign on YouTube was launched on 1 April, playing with the idea of April Fool's Day. The campaign lasted until 5 May, when the occupation took place. It consisted of twenty-seven clips that can be grouped into two main genres: political jamming and political manifesto. Political jamming videos subverted the commercial imagery of the 1980s,[12] while in the political manifesto Macao hosted eminent figures in the cultural world, including the Nobel Prize–winner Dario Fo and theorists Franco Berardi, an Italian activist and philosopher, and Antonio Caronia, a new media theorist. Yet for Caronia, his ties with Macao are more complicated. When he came to Macao he was in the Faculty of NABA (*Nuova Accademia di Belle Arti*) in Milan where he was teaching New Media Aesthetics, and some of Macao's founders and first wave participants were students in his classes. These important figures stressed the importance of Macao and how it was needed in the city. Interestingly enough, although Macao did not officially exist yet, these figures spoke of Macao as if it was already there, acting in the world. This allows us to trace another coupling in the notion of event: that is, its positioning between the actual event happening and its performative/discursive creation. In other words, one question of analysis might be: under which circumstances does an event come into existence in its full power? This issue will be returned to and discussed in the closing section of this chapter.

Third, after the launch of the YouTube campaign, a wheeled video box appeared in the streets and the main squares of Milan. Through it, Macao activists asked the population what their needs and desires were related to Macao. In a similar attempt, the activists made an open call (known as *bando*)[13] to the Milanese population through their newly constructed website (based on Tumblr). People were invited to provide their own interpretation of the acronym of M.A.C.A.O. and to attach to it to their idea of a proposal for a seminar, an event, or a project to be held in Macao. Furthermore, with the notable exception of Facebook,[14] all Macao's main social network profiles were established from 1 April on Instagram, Twitter and YouTube. These profiles displayed a coherent palette of colours and a specifically designed logo where art and knowledge workers visibly employed their skills in the making of Macao. This shows how, from the beginning, Macao was constituted as a brand, not just as a recognisable icon, and to the extent that it served as a device through which communication, effects and values were conveyed and negotiated (Arvidsson 2006).

Finally, the main call for action – the occupation on 5 May – was diffused through a relatively old tool: a mailing list. Two main factors explain the use of a mailing list. The first is related to the heritage that previous mobilisation cultures shared among the enlarged group that, immediately before the occupation, also included members connected with Milanese social centres. The second reveals both the awareness of the privacy and security limits of commercial social media platforms and the availability of independently managed servers or email servers provided by counter-cultural organisations.[15]

## THE GALFA TOWER EVENT

> We need to underline that we are aware that we are inside, that we are not anymore the decorators of the imaginary, as artists have been for a long time, we are inside a mechanism of valorisation, a mechanism of production of imaginary.
>
> —Antonio Caronia, Macao press conference, 5 May

They gathered to occupy the Galfa Tower on 5 May 2012, at 11.00 am, in *Piazzale Lagosta*, a market square in the Isola neighbourhood. The square is at walking distance from the tower and undoubtedly constituted a convenient spot from where to start, but, as I have highlighted in the first chapter, Isola represents a highly symbolic space for Milan because of its history of resistance to gentrification and for hosting the Isola Art Center, where the founders of Macao acquired previous experiences of artistic activism. Once the gathering was complete they started moving. However, it was not a demonstration, nor was it a parade: there were no banners, no slogans were sung and no colourful displays were shown. It was a calm and determined walk towards a precise target with a similarly precise intention: 'We open Macao in order to allow culture to recapture a piece of Milan'.[16] Among the hundreds of citizens who took part in the walk, activists of the local antagonistic social centres scene were also present as well as activists belonging to other nodes of the National Network of Occupied Theatres. People who populated LdA assemblies in the previous months were present and, most importantly, mainstream media were also invited to join and were filming when the activists broke into Galfa Tower. During the press conference, which took place shortly after, at least two national television networks (Sky and La7, Italian television channels) and two national newspapers covered the event. According to an interview conducted for this study with an activist, media contacts had been established in the previous symbolic occupation of the Milanese contemporary art museum. This shows how, in the planning of the occupation, the media were embedded by Macao in their own narration, they were a part of the events planning.

It is important to underline how the planning of the event also involved, from the beginning, the existence of an already fixed number of working groups in key areas that were vital to the development of Macao. In a matter of days, thousands of people visited Macao, and hundreds joined the working groups to carry out video editing, communication – within the organisation as well as a press office who promote the organisation's brand on social media – and gardening, and to commence their own projects. Their neighbours donated plants, while architects and engineers used their expertise to secure and make the space safe for its dwellers. Artists, designers and performers participated and at the same time envisaged the Galfa Tower as a free space, a common place to work and create together. Daily life was disrupted as a conspicuous number of people took leave from their jobs in order to participate in the process of becoming Macao. In this process, identities were shaped. Through the experience of collaborative work, new alliances were built and decisions were taken in assemblies with widespread participation. In a word, solidarity emerged, and this will be the true key for the future existence of Macao, a pillar supporting its relations and a sound background for its construction. These themes will be explored in chapter 4 in relation to the organisation of becoming an institution. A plausible hypothesis for Macao's success lies in the symbolic value of the occupying action, in the bold gamble implied by the choice of occupying a thirty-three-storey building, in a critique of a neoliberal city and providing, at the same time, a believable way out for its citizens.

Returning for a moment to the open call (*bando*) that LdA publicised on the Macao website from 1 April, it was only after the first days of occupation that applications begin to populate their database.[17] Within the month of May, they received 136 applications, for projects ranging from visual arts endeavours, installations, performances, live concerts, to seminars, and so on. The striking thing about these applications is that when applying, using a Google Form, applicants had to specify if their project was a single one-time event, or if its duration was up to a week, a month, or permanent. Of 236 applications received – 90 per cent of which were in May and June 2012 – only 160 specified a duration and, among them, 109 stated that their contribution was to be intended as permanent. This finding is telling, as it shows the needs and the desires that moved the applicants to apply, and the temporal horizon in which they were investing: not to be a single contribution, but to be an active part in the process of becoming Macao.

Within the main event of occupying a skyscraper, those of a different nature took place. A number of leading figures in the political, cultural and artistic worlds visited Macao and publicly attested their full support to the cause, providing additional visibility. Some of these visits were live and free performances, resulting in a massive public interest. Such ambivalence, between an event rooted in a political stance and the event subsumed in the 'economy of the event' represents an ambiguity that deeply permeates the activity of Macao. This will be addressed in the concluding paragraph and, more extensively, in chapter 5 which discusses the economic model of Macao.

The complex mix that I have attempted to describe in these pages was also permeated by a diffuse aesthetic component, as I have noted in my fieldnotes in box 3.1. The lived experience that informs this page of fieldnotes gives an account of how artistic sensibility was embodied in the planning and thinking of the experiential activity Macao proposed and, more generally, in the overall experience of Galfa Tower. Moreover, such initiatives were meant to produce an *aesthesis* in the participants, a commonly shared perception. These notes, which also appeared in a different format in a blog,[18] attest to an individualised and subjective perception, and, probably, sociologically speaking, they lack a certain distance and objectivation: a euphoria that, in those days, was shared by thousands of people connected to Macao through social media.

## BOX 3.1. FIELDNOTES: THE VERTICAL WALKS

Sunday, 13 May. I decide to spend my afternoon in Macao. The schedule of daily cultural activities proposed by Macao to the citizens of Milan is dense. Starting from 3.00 pm, it is possible to take vertical walks up to the 23rd floor. At 5.00 pm, on the seventh floor there is a reading of the sixth chapter of *La Vita Agra* (*It's a Hard Life*), a book by Luciano Bianciardi who, in 1959, sets his story in this very building, Galfa Tower – then the headquarters of a mining company that caused a disaster, involving dozens of casualties, in a rural area of Tuscany, where the author came from before moving to Milan to work in the cultural industry. At 6.00 pm is a theatrical performance on the first floor, and finally at 7.00 pm a general assembly on the ground floor. Meanwhile, thematic roundtables keep working hard: photographers talk about the creation of a shared archive for their shots; the architecture/self-building group sketches an organisational chart which occupies an entire wall. The gardening group plants, flowers and vegetables which neighbours have given to Macao for the creation of an urban garden. I'm impressed by their organisation: communication is efficient, everybody knows everything, information circulates, total openness, hierarchies are subverted by insiders and outsiders. I sign an appeal in favour of Macao (prepared by the famous jurist Ugo Mattei) and I go to the gathering point for the vertical walk. It's 4.30 pm, we huddle around the guide (a Macao activist) who, before starting, tells us the story of the building. Initially, the headquarters for a mining company and an oil company, the building at a later stage hosted a bank (*Banca Popolare di Milan*). Unused for fifteen years, the tower, owned by the Ligresti Group and founded by one of the most discussed Italian lobbyists, was chosen by Macao as space, a container, and symbolic vector for their New Centre for Arts, Culture and Research of Milan. (Here are some reflections of my experience at the heart of the former business centre of Milan [*Centro Direzionale*] about the role of the artistic/aesthetical sensibility in the Macao project.)

The vertical walk allows one to *feel* in one's own body, and legs, the path of social ascent. Through the continuity of these steps, one after the other as opposed to the discontinuity of the elevator, it is possible to connect the up-down connection of this organisation, the manager of the top floors with the receptionist at the first, passing through the white collars in the womb of the building. Macao offers a new point of view both in a metaphorical and in a terribly real way. If I think of the places and the heights of my everyday life I realise that I often move underground, I work and study in a library on the first floor, and I only go to the third to visit the offices of my supervisors. In Paris, I lived more often on the higher floors, but this is no contradiction: in bourgeois buildings, the *bonnes à tout faire*, the domestics or the intellectuals who cannot afford any better housing, live on the top floor. On those floors live students and young couples now. It's interesting to note how most of the time we have to pay to see a city from above, and usually we are disposed to do that when we are in an elsewhere which situates us as tourists, and seldom if ever do we do so in the town where we live. The experience planned and offered by Macao is radically new: providing a critical platform to the Milanese citizenry, calling them to see with their own eyes the city they live in from a different and innovative perspective, not veiled by touristic amusement. In a certain sense, they integrate the territorial knowledge of the city that each one of us possesses – a detailed, deep, living knowledge – with the top-down point of view of the establishment: rough, rational and impersonal.

## MACAO'S MEDIA PRACTICES

Macao's presence on social media is highly diversified and includes Facebook, Twitter and YouTube. At the time of writing, over 53,000 people follow its Facebook fan page. To provide a wider frame, the Occupied Valle Theatre of Rome has 84,000, while the Nuovo Cinema Palazzo has 13,000 followers. Smaller nodes in the network include the Teatro Pinelli Occupato – Messina or the Ex-Asilo of Naples, with 9,400 and 1,700 followers. Macao's fan page was created on Facebook on 8 May 2012, three days after the Galfa Tower occupation. Since then it has *capitalised* on the urban and media effervescence that had coalesced around Macao during the occupation. The total number of users who viewed at least one post published by Macao on Facebook grew from 102,840 on 8 May to 490,000 viewers on 15 May. This constituted their peak of visibility and coincided with Macao's eviction from the tower by the Italian authorities. From that moment onwards, it decreased to 89,000 during the post-eviction period, when they were based at *Palazzo Citterio*, stabilising at a daily average of 30,000 over the following months.[19]A Twitter profile was created on 1 April 2012, and this has around 12,000 followers and 8,000 tweets, with an average of 7 tweets per day. Internal data concerning the Twitter audience is not available, thanks to external databases.[20] However, it is possible to state that the buzz around Macao during its first phase of intense mobilisation followed the same dynamics that characterised the Facebook page. Be that as it may, as the Twitter profile was active from early April, the time of Macao's launch campaign, it is fair to interrogate if and to what extent tweets actually supported the digital aggregation of Macao's constituency. As is visible in the graphic (figure 3.1), during April the number of daily tweets – from and about Macao – range between two and fifteen: a number that is insufficient to explain the subsequent explosion. Deepening the analysis of these tweets, during April the profile's activity was limited to interactions with the other nodes of its theatre network and Macao was incapable of attracting a wider audience, at least digitally. Furthermore, even if we consider the relative peak, around 80 tweets, the day before the Galfa Tower was occupied – when the idea that Milan would soon have an 'artistic' occupation was quickly spreading in the offline world – it appears substantially less intense compared to the 3,000 tweets (produced by or directed to Macao) that constitute the absolute peak during the day of eviction from the Tower. If we consider, for instance, all the hashtags related to Macao on those days (#macao, #tuttisumacao, #iostoconmacao, #torregalfa), it comes to a total of almost 20,000 tweets published during 15 May.

Concerning Macao's YouTube channel: this is comprised of 113 videos with 180,000 views and 671 subscribers. As I have mentioned already, it is this platform that hosted Macao's launching campaign. Twenty-seven videos were produced, starting on 1 April and concluding on 4 May, with a number of views that ranges from 241 to a maximum of 6,673,[21] an average of 1,868 views per video. Finally, if we consider the 50,000 views gathered across the whole campaign, it is plausible that a viral propagation of Macao's message took place on YouTube. What must be taken into account, in this case, is that only 10 per cent of views[22] occurred during the preoccupation phase, proving that the Galfa event induced sympathisers, media professionals or fellow citizens to inform themselves retrospectively about what Macao was about and how it became possible.

Leaving for now the quantitative data, we can present the practices identified in Macao's social media strategy. One point of reference, in this endeavour, is the concept of *media practices* elaborated by Nick Couldry (2012),

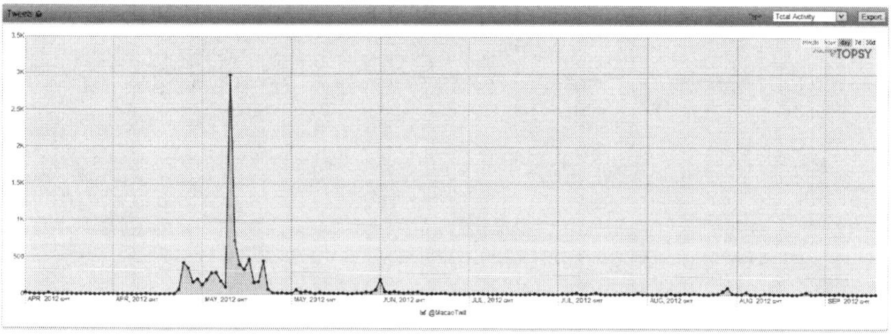


**Figure 3.1 Total Tweets Created by Macao or Directed to Macao, 1 April 2012 to 30 June 2012.** *Source*: Topsy.com.

which makes it possible to identify 'what people do with media in the context in which they act' (Couldry 2012, 35). Following this conceptualisation, media practices are those practices addressed specifically to media; that involve media, but that do not make them their primary object; practices that in order to fully develop rely on a pre-existing media system, or on a specific operation of such a system. Practices are always about regularities: that is, regularities of action; they are a social product and, as such, they embody a shared knowledge, power relations and constraints on action. Based on semi-structured interviews and digital ethnography (Rogers 2013), Macao's social media activity is based on four distinct media practices:

1. Information
2. Announcement
3. Dissemination of imagery
4. Strategic incursions into the media

Information practices refer to the regular and daily diffusion on social media, particularly on Twitter, of a certain number of news items from independent media outlets on themes having an affinity to Macao's identity (e.g. the extensive coverage granted to Gezi Park events in May 2013). The second category includes communications that concern the diffusion of news regarding events organised by Macao or 'service announcements' during mobilisation phases. This kind of activity is performed especially through Facebook. An example of how the dissemination of imagery aims to evoke rather than inform, creating expectations and transmitting an aesthetic mood, is provided by the campaign that preceded the blitz-occupation of the 'Maestoso' Cinema, set up in order to celebrate Macao's first birthday on 5 May 2013. A visual campaign that attempted to arouse interest by foreshadowing the imminent event provided no explanation on its concretisation in the urban space. In this manner, media practices were deployed online, with the aim of producing effects offline. Lastly, strategic incursions that focused directly on the media with the goal of disrupting the symbolic order in the media ecosystem showed a strong affinity with the situationist *détourenment*. A concrete example of this kind of practice was the complex subvertising campaign elaborated to critique the 'big event' of Milan's Design Week held annually in April, complemented by the 'Fuorisalone', which nowadays has become more influential than the former.

To conclude, Macao's social media use appears to have been inspired by a vertical approach (Kavada 2013) and represents a strategic tool in which both the Macao activists' decision-making processes and their organisation culture are not openly involved. For Macao, social media are not spaces in which things 'really' happen – they are, instead, vehicles for making things happen in the real urban space. How can we account for the aggregation around, and in, Macao? Through my quantitative analysis, I have ascertained that social media did not play a fundamental role. However, it is plausible to hypothesise that a role was played by pre-existing networks – both online and offline – to which Macao activists had access. It remains to be clarified in what way available theories in the connective logic paradigm can help us understand the deployment of Macao. What is at stake here is how a particular gaze on reality, the paradigmatic vis-à-vis the pragmatic, also influences the possible interpretation and the significance of what is studied. In other words, the paradigmatic attitude is interested in extracting from reality general trends to inform a new vision of how things work (in our case, political mobilisations mediated by digital technologies). Whereas a pragmatic view, while observing the same phenomena, would be interested in forging a situated comprehension that does justice to the context in which things really happen. This operation has profound consequences on what can be said, and what can be said with validity, about the state of things. What I propose in the following sections is ultimately a case that privileges the pragmatic view as it allows us to assess elements that, in our case, contradict the kind of interpretations that are made at a paradigmatic level.

## CONNECTIVE LOGIC: A PERFORMATIVE DIMENSION

At first glance, the intersection between digital media and Macao's wave of mobilisation appears to be easily readable through a 'logic of connective action' lens. Connective logic is a concept introduced by Bennett and Segerberg (2013) to describe a contentious action characterised by personal action and self-organised networks. The two authors suggest that the most recent cycle of protest by Indignados and Occupy, for example, has been nurtured by connections without organisation, where the structural lack of an organisational scaffold has been balanced by the efficient financing of the private politics of social networking platforms (Papacharissi 2010). Macao's thriving presence on social media and its organisational autonomy suggests a closeness to connective action which distinguishes Macao from most established and traditional protest movements. However, a deeper ethnographic analysis reveals a global picture that is more puzzling and contradictory than expected.

Macao springs into an open and inclusive frame of action that replaces belongingness to a group and strict ideological identification with the fluid openness of human encounters and cooperative planning. However, this structural autonomy does not lead to the 'personal action frame' that Bennett and Segerberg have found to be present in Occupy protests and that are explained by multifaceted individualisation (Ibid., 744). On the contrary, Macao is constantly displayed in the form of a plural subjectivity: anchored to the 'us' of the founding members and projected into the forthcoming 'common constituent field' where idiosyncratic experience will be valued and subsumed in a more general project. Moreover, Macao's social media practices date to the days after the occupation of Galfa Tower: Facebook, Twitter and YouTube profiles were not very popular during the preparatory stage and the first days of mobilisation (and were even absent, as was discussed in the previous section).

Thus, the role of digital media in Macao cannot be traced at the organisational level nor at the symbolic one, at least in the terms identified by Bennett and Segerberg. The constant attempt at building a collective action frame marks a considerable distance with the spreading individualisation of politics embodied by those platforms. The logic of connective action seems not to offer an adequate paradigm by which to understand the richness of communication practices in the deployment of Macao's contentious action. Even if we turn to other analytical models, however, the picture does not become clearer and less ambiguous. For instance, the symmetrical correspondence between internet cultures and strategic/organising/decision-making cultures identified by Kavada (2013) does not seem to apply to Macao, where 'vertical' communication cultures (managed mainly by professionals, hierarchical and event-driven) co-exist with inward-oriented and participatory decision-making cultures (Ibid., 40). During Macao's weekly assemblies, that I witnessed in 2013, the efficiency of its decision-making processes never managed to actively involve all participants nor fully valorise their expressive contributions. On the contrary, the high level of professionalisation in the management of Macao's communication resources, together with the website as a showcase of events rather than as a platform for decisions, reveals a prevailing vertical culture where information flows between all members of an organisation, involving the systematic dissemination of information outside the organisation.

I propose that the eccentricity of Macao, in relation to some of the most far-reaching and comprehensive analytical models available in the recent literature, does not only evidence the quirky peculiarity of this case study. More deeply, it indicates the need to go beyond the surface use of media that seems to be transversally shared by heterogeneous social movements; one that is independent from their specific cultural features and political aims. Away from this apparently common surface, a striking heterogeneity of motivations becomes unearthed: symbolic meanings and functional appropriation find that the roles played by digital media in collective action are as numerous as the number of cultures that use them. It is undoubtedly true that digital technologies, especially social networking sites, can make mobilisation and recruitment more efficient – insofar as they potentiate the symbolic value of messages through personalised framing, and enhance the rapidity of dissemination through networks that, without being political in nature, reproduce and pluralise people's life-worlds. However, the way in which this potential is effectively translated into practice does not necessarily coincide with a strong emphasis on individualisation, nor does it coincide with a full replacement of organisational structure by technology-enabled networks of personalised communication.

The translation of technology into a socio-technical framework is always the outcome of a negotiation between its functions (Hutchby 2001) and the sociocultural contexts in which they are appropriated. As Kavada (2013, 77) shows, cultures of communication which determine how some kinds of uses are actualised and others are ignored, do not develop in a vacuum; rather they are holistically connected to the system of beliefs, values and assumptions that shape the organisations, strategies and decisions of social movements. Yet, the continuum vertical-horizontal used by Kavada to articulate a typology of internet cultures does not cover the broad spectrum of possible convergences between the different layers of cultures that constitute a social movement. This typology appears to be excessively affected by the access-interaction-participation paradigm (Carpentier 2011) that has informed practices and reflections on the political potentialities of digital media.

> In minimal forms, media professionals retain strong control over process and outcome, restricting participation to access and interaction, to the degree that one wonders whether the concept of participation is still appropriate [. . .] In the maximalist forms, (professional) control and (popular) participation become more balanced, and attempts are made to maximize participation. (p. 69)

If the issue of participation is intrinsically pertinent to analyses of political processes and the mobilisation of social movements, one should not presume that it represents the only discriminating factor to assess digital media use by.

Participation is emblematically shown by the case of Macao: notwithstanding the emphasis placed on the experimentation of participatory decision-making processes and the value given to the personal experience of activists, neither websites nor social media profiles have been considered by activists as platforms in which to deploy these participatory dynamics. Within social movements, the multifaceted complexity of the interdependence between technology and culture suggests a need to abandon paradigmatic/classical frameworks in favour of pragmatic/practical analytical models that are open enough to grasp, for each case, the cultural specificity of the technological appropriation at stake.

I propose interpreting the role that digital-networked communication practices play in the mobilisation process through the concept of 'idioculture' (Fine 1979), 'a system of knowledge, beliefs, behaviours, and customs shared by members of an interacting group' (Fine 1979, 734). Idioculture is useful in contextualising communication practices which incorporate the beliefs, values and symbols that shape the broader character and practice of a movement. Its concept is founded on the starting assumption of cultural differentiation between people on aspects such as cultural attire, language, arts, architecture, and religion. Even against a backdrop of common goals, comparable memberships and similar environments, groups develop unique cultures and different styles of behaviour. This uniqueness arises as environmental contingencies are always mediated by idiosyncratic social definitions that emerge during group interaction. Idiocultures are the outcome of the very fabric of social interaction through which a group continuously engages itself 'in the construction of a social reality, a history' (McBride 1975), and a sense of meaning (Berger and Luckmann 1967) (Ibid., 737). This emphasis on cultural differentiation resonates with the main argument of *The Social Shaping of Technology* (Mackenzie and Wajcman 1985), according to which technologies do not exist in their indisputable materiality, but only in the cultural context through which their materiality becomes meaningful for specific groups of adopters.

The concept of idioculture was originally applied by Fine (1979) to the study of baseball teams in the United States, and how teams combined two major elements of group life: task orientation (winning games) with socio-emotional orientation (peer friendship). The extension of this concept to the field of social movements, more specifically to communication practices that mediate their contentious action, requires further refinement. Social movements are a type of social group that are 'defined by actions that take the form of a visible performance' (Dayan 2005, 52). A social movement is thus 'a public' in the sense that has been detailed by Dayan (2005): a social group that requires a public that watches it perform. Public cannot be invisible, it 'must "go public" or it is not a public' (Ibid., 52). Consequently, the elements of a social movement's idioculture I am looking for must include a performative dimension, through which the group enters into a dialogue with, and actively intervening in, the surrounding society.

## EVENTFUL LOGIC: EVENTFUL PROTEST

Analysing the long cycle of protest for global justice, that symbolically started with the Battle of Seattle against the World Trade Organization (WTO), della Porta (2009) proposes that we consider mobilisation and demonstration not just as an effect of a given political opportunity structure and organisational resources, but rather as an event capable of triggering a transformation of the affective, relational and cognitive dynamics of a movement. Inspired by the concept of *eventful temporality* elaborated by Sewell (1996), in which events are defined as occurrences capable of transforming the social structure, della Porta asks that we think in terms of *eventful protest* and focus on those events which, within certain cycles of protest, affect structures by creating new organisational networks, connect pre-existing frames of action and establish new bonds.

Revisiting the results of the analysis I conducted on Macao, it is possible to understand how linking communication practices and artistic production is a shared *eventful logic*. The study of Macao's media practices reveals how online activity mainly consisted of the dissemination of imaginary functional to the deployment of events in the urban space. The occupation of the Galfa Tower, for example, can be considered as a 'big event' in its own right; a surprising occurrence that actualised the unexpected and disclosed unforeseen possibilities.[23]

In line with the founders' desire to oppose the neoliberal logic of cultural events, 'The event is not the solution to predetermined problems, it is rather the opening of new possibilities that pose new questions and solicit the imagination of new replies' (Lazzarato 2005, 13). Macao's first major public act deployed a new meaning of an event, as an opportunity for change, as an insurgence of the unpredictable and an irruption of new generative forces in society. Bringing back to life the inanimate space of Galfa Tower created the conditions in which it was possible to develop a political discourse on the social role of art and on cultural expression, on the value and the practices occurring in communal spaces. At this point we can recuperate the notion of *logic of aggregation* elaborated by Juris (2008, 2012) – a mass of individuals assembling from diverse backgrounds within physical spaces – and apply it to the case of Macao, specifying an *eventful logic* based on the strategic and cultural appropriation of *eventful protest* proposed by della Porta that generates new organisational networks. In other words, the symbolic rupture was triggered by the occupation of the Galfa Tower which provided the context for the legitimation of a new political discourse. Macao's consolidation was based on a deep cultural rootedness capable of interacting with activists' professional competencies and the recreational and convivial habits of the metropolitan public.

In contrast to the *paradigmatic* definitions found in recent literature, I propose a *pragmatic* concept, in which the relevance of digital media for mobilisation *has to be found* in the context in which they are used. It is likely that the eccentricity of Macao, not only indicates its contingent specificity but calls into question the applicability of conceptual categories derived solely from the technological characteristics of media. The risk here being: overwriting the actual significance of media practices (Couldry 2012) with expectations about how they should function according to media theory.

The analysis of communication practices combined with the analysis of Macao's creation has enabled me to empirically establish the notion of eventful logic as the *fil rouge* (red thread) between technological affordances and the structuring of Macao's agency. To conclude, what I would like to suggest for future investigation and verification is not so much a new label: it is, rather, an analytical method in which the role of mediated communication practices is investigated as a dynamic interdependence between the digital tools used, the cultural contexts and the subjects who inhabit them, and their specific skills and strategies.

Even in the stabilisation phase, planning events have continued to play a crucial role in the symbolic mediation of Macao. Their diary over the last year looks like a patchwork of concerts, workshops, theatre performances, meetings and festivals. It is no longer possible to find a coherent discourse about what Macao is on Macao's website, or even what its objectives and its purposes are. Instead, a progressive chain of events is the only discursive production of Macao in recent months when resources for self-narration began to dry up. This development naturally responds to the needs of economic sustainability, but it is also consistent with the professional skills of the people involved, as knowledge workers who are able to set up events and communication campaigns in a very short time. Paradoxically, as revealed through my digital ethnography, the activists themselves have exported their own *eventful language* in Macao, intended as a symbolic framework of the signs and meanings they have learned in the creative industries in which they work and against which they are mobilised.

## *Chapter 4*

# Organising Being an Institution

To pin down Macao's organisational model, the present chapter investigates the organisational and relational aspects of Macao's life and activities. Organisation and relation are two terms that communicate different schemes and political sensibilities. Whereas organising entails a structuring activity aimed at efficacy and goal-attainment, relation constitutes a looser and wider concept that embraces general human relations and the abstract ideas that shape groups, communities and organisations. In this sense, the concept of relation allows room for a political stance. Room that is often used by social movements to redefine new relational modes and, ultimately, to search for a different (and better) life. It is in the chasm between these two concepts that I arrange my analytical space.

Linked to the topics discussed in the previous chapter concerning the eventfulness of Macao's logic of political mobilisation, Macao can be envisioned not as a well-defined organisation that produces events but as a linking point for events. In other words, an event might also act as an organisational device for which Macao does not produce events to persist as an organisation, but exists due to a series of events that through action and communication become the organisation. Within Macao, the issue of organisation is rarely worded in these terms, rather it is framed on relational footings in topics such as care, conflict, embodiment and power distribution. The thematic strand of relation arose from the ethnographic research, but it was during later reflection that I realised that relations ultimately referred to organisational forms. Relation, within Macao, represents a discursive device through which it is possible to manage participation and, most importantly, through which one can tackle, reflexively, the political and ethical issues connected to being an organisation.

The theme of relation is crucial for the life of Macao, regarding its internal and external dynamics. Internally, relations are fundamental as they constitute a field in which struggles are fought in order to establish a hierarchy among two core areas of Macao's activities: action and production. As we will see in the final chapter, relations are deeply interconnected with the logic of action and models of cultural production. Concerning the former, as we have highlighted in the previous chapter, eventful logic draws on bodies acting together on artistic and aesthetic elements that produce strong ties. Concerning the latter, as we will see in the following chapter, the design and the implementation of alternative models of cultural production is often conducted with relations in mind, both as oppositional and supportive elements. Relations, therefore, do not play their roles as if they were confined to two separate realms within Macao because they also act as a hinge internally and externally.[1] To identify the relational mechanics at work within Macao, I will explore three main dimensions. The first tackles the articulation between the individual and the collective level of participation that produces what I define as a *non-exclusive dialectic* between these two levels. The second investigates how participation is organised along with opposed and coexisting notions of horizontality and hierarchy, and analyses the shifting balance between radical inclusion and leadership. The third and last dimension involves collaborative making processes, which help to build and maintain relations and to handle conflicts in a better way. This last dimension is a more background dimension as it is embedded in the first two dimensions and influences, in an encompassing way, Macao's relations.

## ORGANISATION IN HYBRID MOVEMENTS

In the last decade, literature on organisation and social movements has emerged and highlighted the fact that a convergence of organisation and social movement studies should take place (Davies and Zald 2005). As noted by Clemens (2005), however, social movement scholars also demonstrate deep discomfort with the concept of organisation. Conceived as a system of order and authority, it seems incapable of taking into account processes of social change. Growing attention has been dedicated to how activists are able to avoid structures and processes of institutionalisation, with new media playing an important role in providing a non-hierarchical environment. Through connective action (Bennett and Segerberg 2012), social mechanisms characterised by weak ties have allegedly made it possible to overcome the rigidity of collective action, whereas collective action is conceived as a superstructural process that endangers freedom and fluidity.

Issues of power and leadership in movements have been relatively neglected in the last five years. In fact, only recently has a renewed interest in these dynamics re-emerged, countering the overwhelming quantity of contributions that have emphasised the flat and distributed nature of new forms of mobilisation, and therefore marginalising the role of leadership and hierarchy. An indicator of this trend is the latest work of the major sociologist Manuel Castells (2012), which deals with the wave of mobilisation that has sparked globally since 2010. In his previous book, *Communication Power* (2009), Castells dealt extensively with the issue of power. In his most recent book, *Networks of Outrage and Hope* (2012), he conceives 'third spaces' – resulting from the interconnection between occupied urban spaces and digital networks – based on the intrinsically free nature of the online space (Castells 2012, 222). Other studies highlight, however, how digital networks are deeply influenced by mechanisms of verticality, authority and exclusion (Gonzalez-Bailon and Wang 2013; Nunes 2014). Other authors (Arvidsson et al. 2015; Gerbaudo 2015) state that we need to overcome the network paradigm – individuals' environment or context for action provides opportunities and constraints on behaviour – to better understand crowd dynamics – the behaviour and interaction of groups of people – emerging in social media as well as in processes of mobilisation.

Within the literature that recentres our attention on issues of leadership and power in social movements, the contribution of Simon Western (2014) helps us to remember how anarchists like Bakunin, Proudhon and Kropotkin did not have particular taboos regarding dealing with leadership. For them 'individuals and groups take temporary leadership autonomously and on behalf of the wider collective, without assuming a formal position of power or authority over others' (Western 2014, 676). Hence interesting connections emerge between the issues of leadership, entrepreneurship and processes of political mobilisation. Critical management studies have recently brought together these three areas (Swann and Stoborod 2014) from an anarchist point of view – similar to what Gregory Sholette (2011) proposed in the field of art criticism in his analysis of the artistic world as it faces enterprise culture. Particularly relevant is Sholette's understanding of the subsumption (and the mirroring, I would add) of artistic organisational models by enterprises:

> It's not the artist's seemingly transgressive, risk taking non-conformity, but exactly a mode of distributed risk and social cooperation denied by neoliberalism that leads certain CEOs and business thinkers to see artistic methods as near-miraculous models of 'just-in-time creativity'. (Sholette 2011, 43)

From a different angle, social movement scholars interrogate the same nexus that brings together cultural innovation, artistic radicalism and disruption to existing capitalist forms. Davis, in particular, focuses on topological similarities among social movements and enterprises.

> Internally formal organizations would seem to exhibit emergent features and mobilisation processes very similar to those we see in social movement groups. Similarly, in their external relations, formal organizations also would seem to mirror their movement counterparts, participating, as they do, in fluid relationships with other organizations, joining in coalitions, and engaging in political action to affect state policy. (Davis et al. 2005, xiv)

What, then, are these movements? Are they still movements as we used to know them – with the same recruitment and organisational mechanics? Let's be clear, social movement studies have provided extremely valuable insights about social movements; however, as has recently been pointed out, they forgot to include capitalism in the equation (Barker et al. 2013). In the attempt to capture the specificity of movements that embody the heritage of artistic avant-gardes, workers' movements and start-ups, a multiplicity of perspectives must be interwoven. In the Italian and international context growing attention is being paid to cultural and social entrepreneurship, to social innovation, and to peer-to-peer forms of production and organisation (Arvidsson and Peteirsen 2012). At the same time, social movements and squatting centres – buildings taken over for social centre purposes – have radically changed (Prujiit 2013; Moore 2015) – increasingly becoming hubs of cultural production and experimentation rather than spaces of social healing and inclusion.

In this line of thought, we can understand Macao explicitly as the offspring of past generations of activists and their lineage. Yet a partially unfaithful offspring, because what Macao did would have been unthinkable only a decade ago. Macao hybridised the inherited experiences of radical movements from the 1970s and the 1980s with a renewed opening towards society at large. This had been foreclosed to their predecessors due to the specific history of violence and repression they had endured after intense years of unrest. The turmoil of those times is epitomised by the 1977 autonomy movements who were crushed by the judiciary and political repression. The 1980s was a decade in which a generation of activists were persecuted and incarcerated: often with trials marked by exceptional judicial powers. Many notable activists and theorists of that time, including Maurizio Lazzarato, Toni Negri, and Oreste Scalzone, found protection in France (thanks to the so-called Mitterand doctrine that would not expatriate them, in the understanding that the accusations made against them were politically based). The fallout of the 1977 revolts led to a sense of social defeat for activists, in which autonomous squatted spaces started serving as a place to develop radical ideas and forms of alternative life, but also places which allowed for social healing and inclusion in the aftermath of violent and traumatic events. Overall, squatted spaces in those years remained significantly segregated from the rest of society. Willingness to participate in society –

that most of that generation perceived as a violent, capitalist and repressive institution – was at a historical low. Reports and discussions of those years (Moroni et al. 1995) testify to a distrust towards the idea of building alliances with the third sector and freelancers – still an emerging stratum of workers in the late 1980s and early 1990s. This was mostly due to the symbolic need for protestors to affirm their values of integrity, one permitting no compromises. What then explains the attitude we witnessed in the 2010s is the product of a rupture of this ideological core with the understanding that the struggle should continue on the symbolic level by directly transforming society, displaying a more outward-driven attitude rather than the inward tendency typical of previous decades. In other words, hybrid forms are emerging in this complex field, and Macao is certainly one among them.

## MACAO'S COMPOSITE REALITY

> Dust, paint, sweat, smell of sweat, detergents, brooms, dustpans, paper, wood beams, coffee, pasta, couscous, coffee, beer, wine, myrtle, cigarettes, computers, music, books, photographs, songs, dances, assemblies, respect, growth, smiles, rages, fears, hugs, kisses, dreams, passions [. . .] encounters. (Macao 2012b)

This excerpt from Macao's diary was written during the summer camp of 2012. It allows us to understand the material, emotional and symbolic dimensions attached to the making of Macao. Shortly after the occupation of the Exchange (June 2012), Macao launched a Summer Camp.[2] This was a two-month-long initiative to turn the building into a hospitable place for Macao. The diary was published every day for the duration of the Summer Camp and it never bore the name of its individual author (if there was one). The Summer Camp served multiple purposes, and through it, we can see some of the key elements that characterise relations in Macao. First, it satisfied a need to widen and consolidate relations inside Macao.

> I wake up rested, perfumed in a soft and cleaned bed . . . what a strange feeling! It was a couple of weeks that it did not happen . . . if I knew this would not happen anymore, I think I'd go crazy. Yet now, in the comfort and cleanliness of my house I feel trapped, I miss my fellas' laughter, the endless discussions and that sense of community, where everyone gives, for better or for worse, in stress and in joy. And so on riding my horse, wind in sails and wings spread to Macao. (Macao 2012b)

The emotional attachment expressed above, alongside the detachment from private houses as traps which separate people from each other, the need to continue the flow started in Galfa Tower, the enthusiasm, the desire to make a space your own, to live collectively under the same roof for weeks, abandoning routines and comfort – all of this constitutes a concrete sign of what the lived experience of Macao meant for its activists and collaborators. In an interview conducted later, this period of intense work was retrospectively acknowledged as a 'golden age, during which Macao was genuinely driven by desire' (MI 4). During this first period, the people in Macao who had technical skills organised the work (see fig. 4.1) so that others could learn conducting tasks which were not always intuitive, immediate or safe. This is exemplified in operations that saw the renovation of a whole rooftop (see fig. 4.2), or fixing the water system, including the heating and energy supply of a four-storey building with dozens of rooms extended over thousands of square metres. A process like Macao's, started by artists, becomes entangled with craft, in a process in which – from the de-materialisation of art, passing through the relational and social wave – it becomes a living process that is deeply rooted in everyday practice and largely outside institutions, and in a process of active drift from them. Being 'captured', to use Deleuzian jargon, does not really matter here, since the starting point of Macao's political action

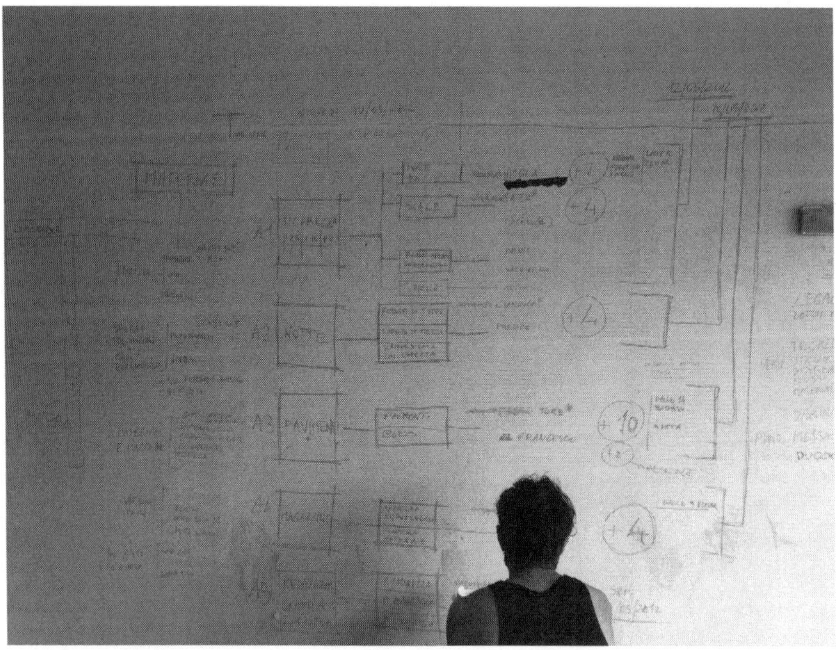

**Figure 4.1 Differentiation of Tasks and Organisation in Macao.** *Source*: Created by author.

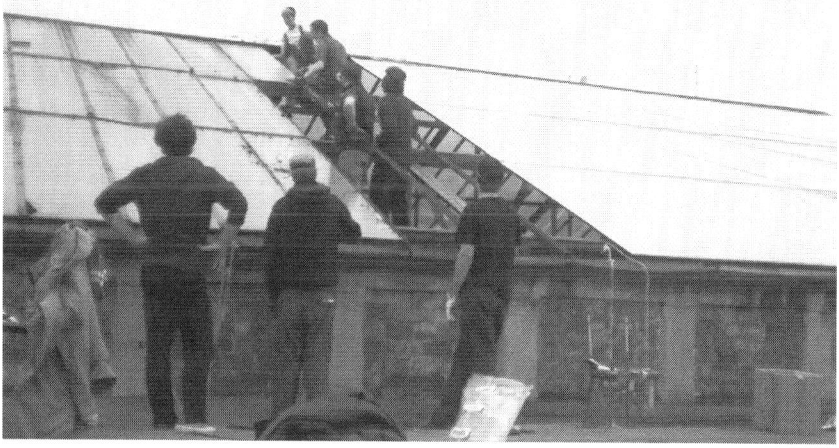

**Figure 4.2 Activists Fixing the Rooftop of Macao** *Source*: Still from YouTube.

is that we all are already subsumed in broad social-structural organisations, such as economics and politics.

The Summer Camp, more pragmatically, served the functional imperative of improving the quality of the space and re-signifying the space itself, a task that was achieved with a particular aesthetical/political frame in mind. To better describe this frame, I combine an ethnographic with a historical analysis, finding substantial analogies with the ideas previously developed by the Isola Art Center – where some of the Macao founders were involved (and are still involved, in some cases) – in clear opposition to the practices of the institutional art world. Their idea was to have a space labelled as a *dirty cube* – opposing the neutral white cube widespread in museums and exhibitions – expresses their refusal of a denaturalising aestheticisation of the occupied space. In other words, to create a New Centre for Arts and Culture that intends to host and produce alternative art and culture (or, at least, do it in a different way) one must make it perceivable in aesthetic and architectural terms. This meant leaving the marks of abandonment visible, in June 2012 in the Exchange, to apply a selective political/aesthetical judgement according to which it appeared legitimate to reveal the marble – covered in a dull white paint – that framed some of the doors but, at the same time, to avoid the temptation to paint anew entire rooms.

Second, the notion of *fight-specific*, underlying the cultural and artistic processes taking place in the occupied space, must take into account local needs. In this sense, re-signifying that space establishes a dialogue with neighbourhood, to organise initiatives and explorations of the vast area that surrounds it (e.g. walks in the abandoned slaughterhouse at the Exchange), making the walls of the Macello speak, and porous to contamination from the outside. Third, and finally, the idea of a *dispersed centre:* that is, conceives of the art centre not as a physical space, but rather as a mental and bodily attitude (Isola Art Center 2013).

Furthermore, the Summer Camp expressed a will to establish Macao as a positive and constructive force of the city of Milan. In this respect, Summer Camp can be viewed as one of the first projects developed in the Exchange, through which a part of the Milanese citizenry was implicated. More precisely, it provided those stuck in the city – due to the traditional Italian summer break in August, during which cities are deserted – with an alternative way to learn new things (e.g. music editing, masonry, restoration), and to cooperate, to work and to be part of something. It is interesting to note that all of these aspects, although subject to a constant process of becoming and change, were also present in the initial project of what Macao should and could have been, as established by the 'founders'. In fact, in a YouTube video created for the launch campaign in April 2012 the autonomist intellectual and activist Franco Berardi, 'Bifo', clearly states that occupying should not constitute an end in itself and what has to be done goes way beyond that. In his words:

> It's not about occupying the streets, although we will continue to do it, it's not to ravage London [. . .] blocking factories and the daily death [. . .] It is about the fact that, while we do all this, we must be aware that the soul of the problem is . . . the soul. It is the collective body, our ability to return to live and express solidarity. Solidarity is not an ethical or a political value, solidarity is the problem of living next to the body of the other, solidarity is the awareness that my interest is the same as the others, solidarity is the pleasure of living in the city as a place where we are together. This is what we have to do, rebuild solidarity, and to do that, Macao: burn banks, set London and Athens to fire, block roads, occupy the factories – of course, if all this is necessary. But maybe what is essential is the word, the sign, the dream, the imagination, in every possible way.[3]

The relevance of Berardi's comment is multipurpose. Although originating from a pessimistic analysis of contemporary society[4] he focuses on solidarity to stress how only together might we eventually overcome our 'sad times'. This is the same trajectory that was followed and experienced by Macao activists, sick as they were of the depressive self-pity widespread in the previous assemblies of precarious workers in which they had participated. His words also signal the performative role of the intellectual discourse on the shaping of a movement. Macao was not yet born when Berardi uttered those words and it is noteworthy how his contribution was embodied in the concrete activities of Macao – if we consider how intensely Macao worked on their imaginary. This heritage shows us once more the deep affinity of Macao with the theorists of the previous generation.

The fact that it was possible for Macao to secure the endorsement of influential public intellectuals reveals the peculiar social status of Macao's founders: a *marginal elite* within the Italian cultural realm, bearers of a high cultural capital, with middle-class backgrounds who directly took part, often with highly visible roles, in the previous waves of mobilisation at national and international levels. It was due to the previous connections already established by the founders of Macao that they could reach the cultural and intellectual panorama necessary for it to be a success. This is a sort of co-belonging that ties not only Macao activists to leading figures of critical thought but to institutional actors in the city of Milan.

Relations in Macao, then, are sites of affect, a fundamental political space in which bonding happens, a space emphasised by activists as the true space in which activism is based. The worthiness of a political endeavour must be evaluated on the quality of such relations, and not on the results attained. Or perhaps it should not be evaluated at all – it must be lived, in all its complexity, joy, disorientation, but also its conflicts. Macao, as a composite reality, partially reflects the complexity of society, and with it bears the marks of some of the traditional cleavages that affect our societies more globally. The next section will deal with such conflicts.

## RESOLVING CONFLICTS

As Macao activists have experienced, being part of a movement – even of a movement where a deep solidarity is successfully built and where collective endeavours are substantial – does not automatically mean that conflicts that flow through the social body of a movement will be overcome. It is in the latency phase of a movement that the typical euphoria – or sense of urgency – leaves room for an everyday-ness (although revolutionised, or in the conscious attempt of being revolutionised) and for reflexion within and across the movement. This process has to be considered with regard to the changing composition of Macao. Starting from the relatively homogenous group of Macao's founders, hundreds of people joined the process in the 'normalised', organisational, phase which coincided with the occupation of the Exchange. After June 2012, not only artists were present but also cultural workers, in the widest sense, incorporating video-makers, employees, students, plus a smaller group of squatters with more technical and manual skills. What is relevant for the present chapter is to unpack how the cleavages that ran through this new composition were addressed, politically and organisationally, by Macao.

Conflicts emerged around the issues of gender, the digital divide and material vs. immaterial work. Differences among participants were not overlooked. As conflicts arose, assemblies were dedicated to the discussion of issues, and in some particularly relevant cases, seminars and meetings were organised. Gender, at least in numeric terms, is not an issue for Macao. The overall composition of Macao shows a substantial equity in terms of male and female distribution with twenty-six males and twenty-four females present in December 2012 (Macao 2012a). What was at stake, then, were the imbalances in roles and functions within the organisation. During my ethnography, I was able to grasp how a perceived unease arose among the activists regarding male dominance in the assemblies. For instance, during a seminar in March 2013, called *Occupare il conflitto* (occupying the conflict), Macao activists pointed out how males were more likely to take their talking turns during the assemblies and to speak longer; they were also much more likely to occupy the public sphere, such as in national or public meetings. During this seminar, led by Federica Giardini, a feminist and political philosopher from the University of Rome, the situation was revealed to be far more complex as it emerged that relations were not determined by gender belonging per se, but rather attitude. Like Angelo, an activist, says in his intervention during the seminar:

> It has not to do with being male or female, it relates with a masculine or feminine attitude. Here in Macao there are female people who have masculine attitudes, they shut me up within the assemblies, and I cannot take the floor [audience laughs] because they have this attitude. Therefore it is reductive to say that in Macao assemblies, or in the national and public meetings, only men can speak, it is about a masculine attitude. (Macao 2013)

It is not that women have no voice in Macao: they express it in different ways and using different channels, one of which being digital social media. Using digital methods and techniques (Rogers 2013), I analysed the flows in the ‘Communication Mailing List’ (CML) used by Macao. This mailing list was initially dedicated to the discussions of the group that was in charge of Macao’s external communications. Later on, this list came to host a number of different topics and it has come to serve as a hub, with multiple functions. First, activists use the list to post news from media outlets and ask for support or additional work to make news publishable in Macao’s social media channels. Second, together with the online platform on WordPress, the CML constitutes a vibrant space of discussion concerning the assemblies and their agenda, and for sharing information that is relevant to the life of Macao (e.g.

public calls, news from the national network of Occupied Theatres, news concerning the global social movement scene, etc.).

The data extracted from the CML amounts to around 3,000 emails which span the period from June 2013 to June 2015. The mailing list data has been elaborated using Gephi,[5] an open-source visualisation tool, which allows us to understand to what extent women occupy Macao's communications. Among the top ten contributors, we find only three men. More significantly, the first contributor, Camilla, shows a degree of engagement that appears to be more than twice (weight=1337) that of the second most active user (weight=668).[6] Ethnographic insight gathered during the fieldwork allows us to understand that Camilla has acted as the 'head' of Macao's communication since the organisation's creation. This information is represented graphically in figure 4.3 by the thickness of the edge that connects her to the central node, which represents the CML itself. Analysing interactions from the mailing list data more closely, greater activity by an individual does not necessarily correlate with the influence of their node. Influence is based here on betweenness centrality,[7] a metric that indicates to what extent a person acts as an intermediary between two other people in the group. This metric is represented by the size and the darkness of a person's node: the darker and the bigger the node, the more influence a person holds in the group.

As is clear in the next graphic (figure 4.4), there is no linear correspondence between a person's activity and their influence. In particular, two males (Emanuele and Ferdinando) and one female (Vittoria) emerge as influencers. These new subjects emerge, showing a substantially lower activity coupled with a higher influence. How is it possible to explain this discrepancy? Following mailing list data, it is revealed that these three people have been engaging in email conversations with a wider number of participants, and are therefore acting as connectors among different subgroups. Emanuele and Ferdinando were also part of the initial group that founded Macao, while Vittoria has been a very active member of the Macao theatre group and has therefore engaged in discussions with them as well as linking their discussions to the main group. Therefore, I suggest that influence also reflects the social dynamics occurring in Macao's offline activities.

This brings us to Macao's digital divide issue. Notwithstanding the high degree of media literacy, typical of knowledge workers (people whose job is to 'think for a living'), Macao's digital tools are not used by the whole of its constituency. There are two main reasons for this phenomenon: those that live in the building (dwellers) and the online realm. First, Macao is at present a relatively small group of people dwelling in the occupied building. They live there due to material need or, in a few cases, as a political choice or for security reasons. Since the beginning, the policy in terms of dwelling has been highly debated. In their first occupation of the Galfa Tower skyscraper,

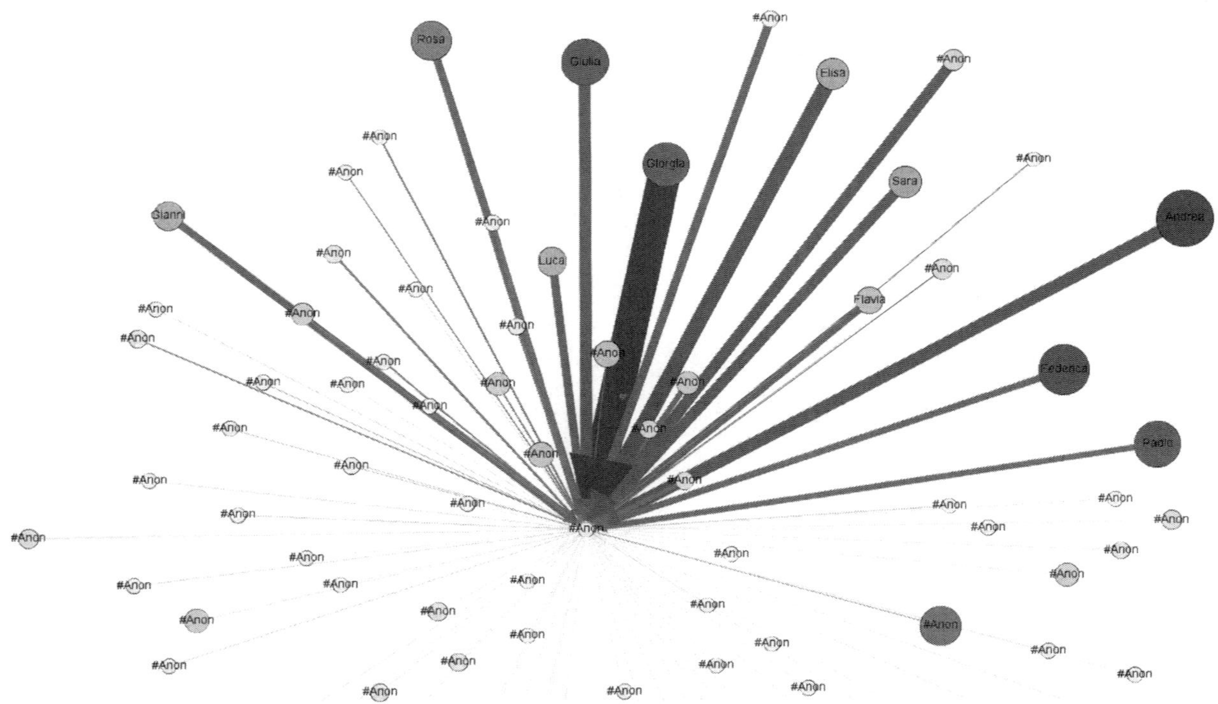


**Figure 4.3 Graph of Communication Mailing List.** *Source*: Created by author.

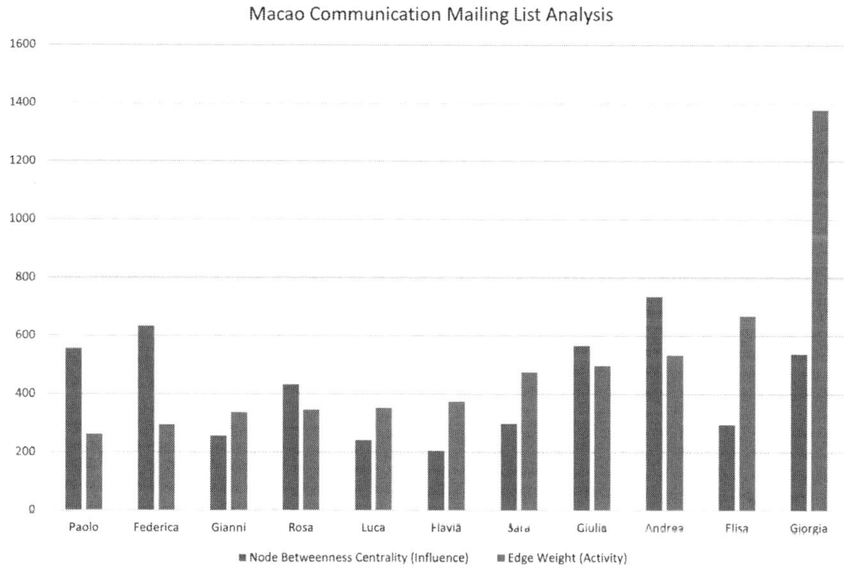


**Figure 4.4 Analysis of CML.** *Source*: Created by author.

people slept there in order to be present in high numbers to resist eviction. While at the Exchange, where Macao is currently based, people dwell in the building in a sort of unlawful behaviour related to Macao's very informal policies. This is tolerated because most of these people would not have the means to sustain the costs of private housing and because they provide a number of technical and manual services which are vital to Macao's economy and cultural activity. It is important to note that this small group of five people neither uses the social digital platforms provided by Macao nor engages in most of the deliberative bodies – namely, the weekly assemblies and the working groups.

Second, another kind of digital divide concerns Macao's online realm. This is related to the internal diversification of platforms (see table 4.1) implemented for internal communication or geared towards intra-organisational ends. We can distribute these tools according to whether they are inclusive or exclusive. These two latter categories can be considered in relative terms, in which the extremes are total inclusion and complete secrecy. Note that personal texts sent via mobile phone or personal emails were excluded for technical and ethical reasons, both digital and ethnographical.

Third, in terms of material vs. immaterial work, to build a visual space of Macao's constituency, a tentative systematisation of the differences that segment Macao's body can be drawn using two axes. The first axis represents artistic skills (AS), while the second axis accounts for communication

**Table 4.1 History of Communications within Macao**

| *Time Period* | *Inclusive* | *Exclusive* |
|---|---|---|
| April–May 2012 | Facebook groups (100+ members) | Mobile phones |
| June–Dec. 2012 | WordPress platform (self-registration, no invite required) | Mailing list of each working group |
| Jan. 2013–Sept. 2014 | CML + WhatsApp (global chat, 100+ members) | WordPress platform (invite only + more exclusive groups are created within the platform itself)/WhatsApp for each working group |
| Sept. 2014–current | CML | WhatsApp abandoned |

skills (CS). The intersection of these two axes produces four ideal types of activist at the inter-linkage between competences and communication (see figure 4.5). The first, showing a high degree of AS and a lower degree of CS can be defined as the 'pure artist': a person who is not particularly keen on manual and technical tasks, whose contribution is artistic (e.g. performing or organising artistic events in Macao). The second category is the 'artistic communicator', and includes the people in Macao that have AS but are willing to transpose their skills into ideas that can be circulated in digital space (e.g. setting up a campaign artistically inspired to be diffused on Macao's Facebook page). The third category, the 'technical communicator', represents all those activists who contribute to Macao's official communication, but not necessarily by deploying highly creative processes.[8] Activities in this area are closer to public relations and also include the sharing of artistic content through social media. Finally, the fourth category, the 'technical activist', is a residual category composed of subjects who show a low degree of both sets of skills whose contribution to Macao lies in their manual/technical work. This fourth category partially overlaps with the dwellers group; aside from being a highly stylised category, it also functions to produce a difference from which the meaning of the other three categories derives. To clarify, inspired by the conceptual sensitivity of Max Weber's sociology, I mean that their positionality is more complex than I am portraying as it has been abstracted and rendered in a more extreme way for analytical purposes, so that the difference and meaning of the categories could emerge more clearly. For example, Weber (2019) highlighted in *Economy and Society*, originally published in 1921, how social class is more about how much money people have if we also factor in people's life chances affected by economic conditions (job availability, nationwide/international production and consumption) and cultural conditions (language, family, social networks, etc.).

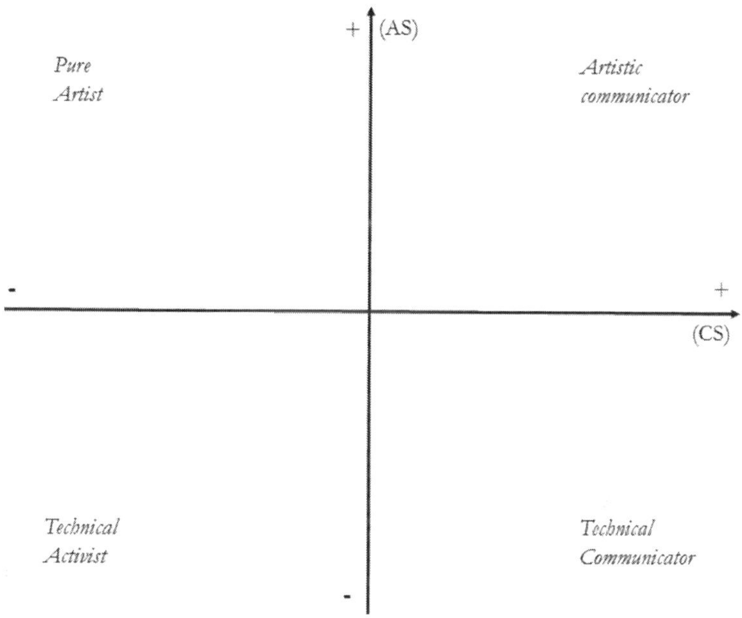


**Figure 4.5 Macao Constituency Ideal Types**. *Source*: Created by author.

For every classification, the same actor at different points in time can play various categories/roles: a choreographer can act as a pure artist when she invents a performance to be staged in the urban space. She can become an artistic communicator by setting up a creative campaign based on that performance.[9] She might be a technical communicator when she tags people online to secure higher visibility of a creative campaign, and, finally, she can be a technical activist when she repairs the floor of the room in which the choreography has been rehearsed. This is not to say that I am invalidating my own typology, since there is an empirical truth supporting it insofar as these different ideal types mirror social and cultural cleavages among the rank and file of Macao, as I have highlighted in chapter 2. The activist I have described, capable of embodying the four different roles, represents a normative ideal that has been explicitly criticised within Macao. In the life of Macao, the ideal activist is someone dedicating resources and time to individual and collective projects created within the movement and, most importantly, is capable of responding to the four ideal audiences that scrutinise their work from every corner. These imagined audiences have different sets of expectations; for example, a communicator must be efficient, the artist must be inspired and display out-of-the-box thinking. This means that the ideal Macao activist must respond to a certain idea of engaged political art (see Making Sense of

Macao), show a high effectiveness and originality in her digital engagement, and conform to a hard-working stereotype when it comes to sharing content or performing manual work for Macao. More specifically, the activist must not just respond to these normative requirements or ideal-typical audiences, but they must also appear worthy of their co-belonging, in the eyes of the different subgroups that populate Macao.

Essentially, very few people in any organisation can perform multiple roles at the highest standard in terms of quality and/or commitment. What appears relevant in terms of conflicts within Macao is that if some immaterial workers tend to have at least the basic resources to perform clerical or manual tasks, the contrary is rarely the case. This helps us to connect the division between immaterial and material workers with another issue: that of leadership. In other words, given the higher accessibility of competences required to perform manual skills compared to the soft skills,[10] the immaterial worker is more likely to get closer to the normative ideal prevalent in Macao. The picture within Macao is more complex, because, as I have experienced in my ethnography, this does not simply result in sheer domination during conflict resolution. In fact, it is thanks to the peculiar organisation model created and incessantly reinvented by Macao that effective counter powers are possible. We will say more about this at the end of the chapter but, before that, it is necessary to say something about Macao's concrete experiences.

## RELATIONS IN PRACTICE

In order to assess Macao's organisational model, I will look now at their cooperative practices and the relations implicated in them. I will present two cases that differ in a number of aspects, which will help to highlight the specificity of Macao's organisation.

### BOX 4.1. CASE 1: REBUILDING THE ROOFTOP

Since the occupation of the Exchange, improvements have been constantly in progress or on the agenda. One major project dealt with the rooftop, the condition of which meant that rain poured into the building and presented the risk of pieces of heavy glass falling into the main hall of the building where the most popular events hosted by Macao take place. In practical terms, the work consisted of removing the old glass plates – which weighed about 30 kilograms – and substituting them with new and lighter polycarbonate panels. The roof condition was known since the first day of the occupation, in June 2012, and it is telling that the press release and the video were released in June 2014, shortly after the work had been accomplished.

Period of work: eight months
Cost of materials: €7,000
People involved: eight per day, on average
Days worked: thirty, on average per person

It took sixteenth months to reach the necessary conditions in order to start the repair operation. It is not that the roof repair was not a compelling task, but rather the proliferation of other projects and urgent duties constantly competed in the list of goals to be achieved. Furthermore, the substantial amount of financial resources needed, €7,000, was also a major cause of delay, since an organisation like Macao does not dispose of that amount of money at any single given moment. This implied a slow but constant allocation of funds in order to buy the necessary materials. It must be noted that none of the activists received remuneration for this project.

There were, on average, eight people involved. These included members of the former self-building working group, some from the dwellers' group and artistic activists who were familiar with technical work. One person, usually the most competent or bravest, was harnessed and worked from the inside to detach the glass plate from the roof structure while a team of three people was dedicated to slowly removing and sliding the heavy glass to the group standing next to them on solid ground. The group coordinated mainly face to face and through personal social media (WhatsApp). In fact, no discussions about this project were conducted in mailing lists or in the WordPress platform. Two more relevant features of this project, useful when seeking to pin down Macao's organisational model, consist in its drive (a material need sustained by the consensual agreement of the assembly), and its inward orientation, since it aimed to take care of Macao's own space.

Once more, the video produced to document the rooftop repair allows us to connect the level of physical work to a discursive level – in this case analysing its translation into a visual narration. The video was edited so as to produce a time-lapse sequence, a technique that renders the passing of time considerably faster. On the one hand, this technique helps to shrink a long activity into a few minutes of video; on the other hand, it is used to contrast the lyrics of the song that plays throughout the whole video. The choice of the song and its lyrics is telling of the activists' approach.

The author, Enzo del Re, was a radical singer who was active in the late 1960s and early 1970s, who had been trained as a classical musician but always refused to play normal instruments, and instead drummed rhythms on a chair to accompany his voice; he requested the minimum pay of a metalworker for his performances. Enzo del Re's political stance was close to post-workerism (a shift away from mass production to a space liberated from capitalist oppression) and Italian political 'autonomy' (independence from the capitalist state and economy) which also constitutes Macao's background.

## BOX 4.2. CASE 2: 'NON È MICA LA LUNA' CAMPAIGN

In July 2013, the Ligresti family, whose financial group legally owned the Galfa Tower skyscraper, occupied by Macao the year before, was subject to three arrests for bankruptcy.[11] These arrests triggered a strong and immediate reaction in Macao. One group thought it was the perfect chance to regain possession of the tower, now legitimised by the arrests of former owners. This project was discussed by a small group through personal media (WhatsApp, phone calls) and a closed mailing list; only hours afterwards did it reach the official mailing list, in which a lively debate took place. During the day, the majority of Macao activists were busy with their day jobs, so a long conversation within the common platform (ninety-nine posts) took place: another small group countered the idea of re-occupying the tower. They agreed that something must be done, that there was a desire to do so, and that the best way to further discuss it was to meet physically. Performing a content analysis of the ninety-nine posts that compose the discussion about re-occupying the tower, I have isolated six main discursive elements: (1) an orientation towards action (Galfa, action, tower, make, com'on, forward); (2) an orientation towards relation (Macao, are, we, we want, we have, we do, we think, common); (3) a regrouping of words that delineate an analytical stance (regulation, Ligresti, prosecutor, speculation, contents, issue, proposal); (4) an organisation of spatial matters and the time frame (now, here, tomorrow, city, moment, space, the Exchange, Milan, square, day, evening, tonight); (5) the modes of action (photo, saying, occupation, to build, to go); and (6) a reflexive take (it would, but, it might, consider, it could).

The content analysis of this discussion allows us to empirically grasp the plurality of needs and orientations that coexist in Macao. What happens, then, is that those who propose re-occupying are, in the first instance, obliged to enter into a dialogue with the whole Macao constituency. Second, the dialogue takes place in the digital environment where their position is not countered but evaluated, commented on and included with a number of other projects that could take place instead of the re-occupation. The conclusion of this dialogue was that the matter necessitated a face-to-face meeting where the group proposing to occupy would face a larger group that had started to support a public campaign. The result of this nightly discussion was to abandon the re-occupation idea because of material difficulties and because it was also perceived as having a limited political impact. The consensus arising from this meeting around the campaign was not a sign of repression of the desires of a minor radical fringe, it rather represented the capacity of the other group's desires to spread to the whole assembly. The result of this exchange was that a campaign was established, and divided into two main actions. The first aimed to denounce the abandonment of a number of buildings in the city of Milan. A quote from Macao's press release (see figure 4.6) clarifies the meaning of this first action:

> Imagine that we feel naked, but we have nonetheless the strength to speak, to write, to point at, to enlarge the meshes of this fabric and to blow up its contradictions.[12]

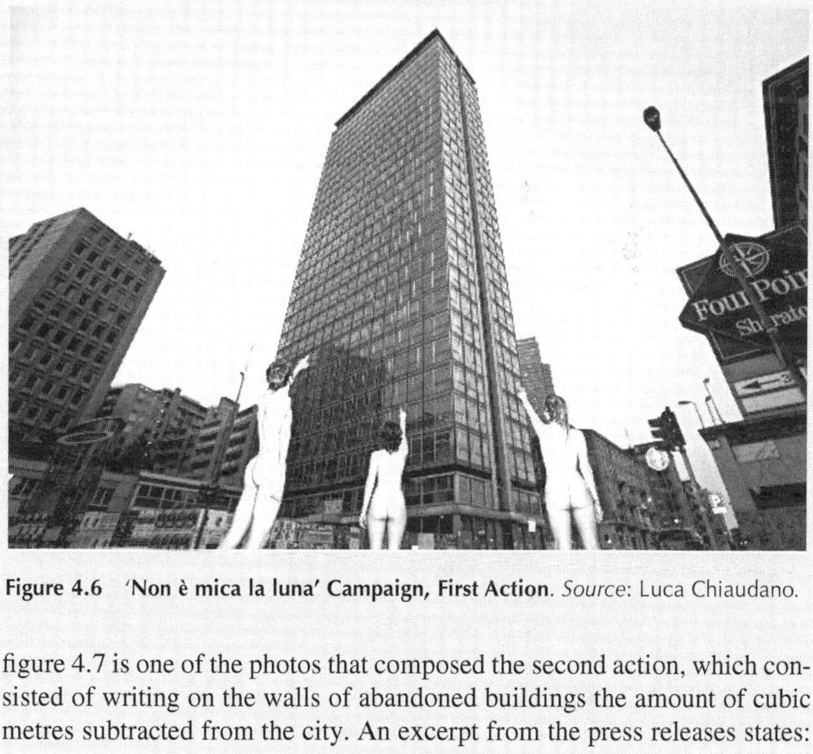

**Figure 4.6 'Non è mica la luna' Campaign, First Action**. *Source*: Luca Chiaudano.

figure 4.7 is one of the photos that composed the second action, which consisted of writing on the walls of abandoned buildings the amount of cubic metres subtracted from the city. An excerpt from the press releases states:

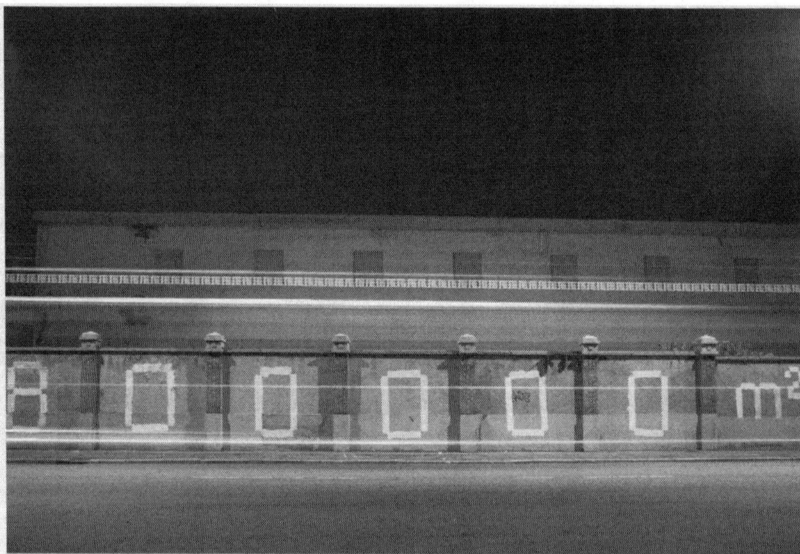

**Figure 4.7 'Non è mica la luna' Campaign, Second Action.** *Source*: Luca Chiaudano.

> Towers, buildings, abandoned areas: the strong deed to leave a mark on these places is meant to expose the physical dimension of the subtraction of space that, until today, was repressed. But the city does not end with abandonment or speculation; it's the possible space for dreams, and represents a geography of desires. Places become then much more than their walls, their matter; they are symbols and they open imaginares. *Non è mica la luna* is the tale of these two cities: the one of abandonment and the one of desire. The first has to be revealed, the second must be staged.[13]

Different elements in this campaign are of interest to understand Macao's organisational model. First, the campaign was based on a compulsive work rate, since the news of the Ligresti family arrest happened on 17 July and the campaign was on Macao's social networks and website thirty-six hours later. It was radically inclusive: every subgroup of Macao felt compelled to give their contribution to a shared and desired goal. Furthermore, it was highly participative and was mediated not just by the assembly but by the online WordPress platform, as well as mailing lists. The drive of the campaign can be identified in a desiring mechanic sustained by small groups who attempt to contaminate others. I personally witnessed the meeting prior to the second action where, at 2.00 am, it was decided to go and write on the buildings with white paint. The number of people willing to participate was so high (around twenty people) that a cap had to be imposed allowing only the people strictly necessary (six people) to perform the job, in order to avoid attracting too much attention from the police patrolling the streets of Milan. Finally, the campaign showed an outward orientation to the extent that it was not about taking care of Macao's own space, but it was rather about taking care of the city.

To conclude the analysis of this empirical case in which relations were embedded, I will look at the interplay with its discursive emergence, which, in this particular case, allows us to say something more about leadership in Macao. Following the arrests of the Ligresti family, the Italian justice minister had been under immense pressure to resign over claims that she had interfered with the transfer out of prison of financier Giulia Ligresti, the daughter of the real estate magnate.[14] What happened next is that Macao, who since its forced eviction from the Galfa Tower suspected the Ministry itself backed the entire operation in order to favour the interests of the owners found footage in its archives that showed a police officer openly stating that the eviction was being carried out because of 'orders from the top', referring to the minister herself. The footage was released on YouTube[15] and triggered a chain reaction, attracting the attention of two national broadcasters who eventually invited Macao to contribute to their prime-time shows, which were covering the Ligresti affair. In the assembly called to discuss this situation, a problem was raised concerning who should represent Macao and voice their critique. The natural choice was Emanuele, one of Macao's founders who had been considerably more exposed to media than others, but another activist openly challenged what he felt was a hegemonic position. Emanuele's leadership on this matter was questioned but, in the end, based on his greater knowledge of the issue, plus his previous experience as a speaker, he was granted renewed, if temporary leadership, until further questioning.

These two cases represent two ways in which Macao acts and in which relations are implicated in very different ways (see also table 4.2). Before we deal with how such different relational modes are able to coexist, I will briefly trace a genealogy of Macao's cooperation. One major element pushing Macao activists to act in such a cooperative way is a critique of the existing competitive relations in the creative industries in which many of the Macao activists live and work. Nevertheless, such a critique does not result in a paralysing effect as occurred in the previous wave of mobilisation on precarity (see Rethinking Art). As we know from Howard Becker (1984) and Bourdieu (1996), art is intrinsically a collective and social activity and therefore is seldom the result of an isolated genius. However, what made possible the

**Table 4.2 Comparing Two Campaigns**

| *Rebuilding the Rooftop* | *'Non è mica la luna' Campaign* |
|---|---|
| Slow work rate | Dynamic and compulsive work rate |
| Social division of labour | Inclusion of everyone |
| Planned activity | Eventful activity |
| Face-to-face coordination and personal social media | Highly participative and mediated by the common platform and the assembly |
| Drive: material need sustained by a consensual agreement in the assembly | Drive: desire sustained by small groups who try to contaminate others |
| Inward orientation (taking care of their 'home') | Outward orientation (taking care of the city) |

complex and collective 'living work of art' that is Macao, was the experience of Galfa Tower (see chapter 3). The solidarity sparked in those early days is still, according to Macao activists, the main source of trust and mutual cooperation despite actors' differing artistic backgrounds. This point is close to the argument put forth by Judith Butler in her essay 'Bodies in Alliance' about the political protest of Tahrir Square, Cairo (Butler 2011). Another element derives from the post-workerist tradition, which has deeply influenced Macao (see Rethinking Macao). To elaborate on this it is interesting to read a quote from the first book published by a small and independent publisher, recently founded by three Macao activists. The book is by Maurizio Lazzarato and it deals with Duchamp's peculiar refusal of work:

> The anthropology of workers' refusal is anchored to an anthropology of labour [. . .] while the idle action (founded on the otium of the ancient) undermines the foundations of the work, it shakes not only the identity of the manufacturer, but also their sexual assignments. What is at stake is the anthropology of modernity: the subject, the individual, the liberty of men, the universality of men. (Lazzarato 2014, 15; my translation)

These thoughts on labour are deeply connected with the substantial import of feminist theory within Macao, in particular, in the politics of difference, a movement of subtraction and creation at the same time, based on the work by the feminist movements of the 1970s on relations (Lonzi 1978). The strong presence of women in the construction of Macao has moulded the movement's forms of action, giving essential importance to the quality of exchange rather than the result it is desired to attain, thus affirming the crisis of the whole business management ideology. This ideology is widespread in many projects of self-entrepreneurship in the creative industries (Bandinelli and Arvidsson 2013) with which Macao has established a non-dogmatic dialogue, unlike its predecessors – such as the centres active in Milan since the early

1980s. A further contribution comes from the work of Alberto Melucci, and his insights about the specificity of women's contributions to social movements. In the excerpt below, he is referring specifically to the feminist movements of the 1970s, yet I find his analysis fits perfectly with the feminine sensitivity embodied in Macao.

> 'Female' activities within the movement consist of pointless meetings, writing for its own sake not for the market, apparently aimless communication, and time spent in ways incoherent with utility and efficiency. The cultivation of memory; the search for the margins, nuances, and seams of experience; and the duplication of the same activities by a myriad of groups, with complete disregard for economies of scale, are all aspects that the dominant masculine culture judges as 'senseless'. Nevertheless, it is this waste that breeds innovation, as recent years have shown. (Melucci 1994, 120–121)

## MACAO'S RELATIONAL PATTERNS

The first finding on Macao's relational pattern is what I define as a *non-exclusive dialectic* between the individual and the collective places Macao's relational pattern beyond the two main available frames of collective and connective action. Through the results of the enquiry presented in this chapter we can see how individual desires and needs are welcomed and find their expression in a dynamic interaction which does not always entail the approval of the assembly (see figure 4.8, mode 4), similar to what happens with the tasks carried out by the working groups. Such desires arise both from people who are already active in Macao and from people who enter Macao for the first time.

Coordination in Macao does not take place in the way that it does within institutions such as unions. Coordination in Macao is a mobile, open and conflicting network in which the different types of associations (working groups, assemblies, alliances, friendships, etc.) constitute spaces for the discussion, and the production of skills, behaviours and expressions in constant transformation. Both the reproduction of the beliefs and moral principles that are derived from the public opinion of the majority and the most innovative political and aesthetic practices find their place here. How, then, has this model been imagined and implemented? Three main elements come together. First, as I have highlighted in the genealogy of Macao's cooperation, previous experiences and orientations inspired the model: art as a social activity, feminism, post-workerist tradition and the 'Galfa effect'. Second, ongoing experimentations by Macao in its activity constantly generated new crossings[16] by other subjects and ideas (see figure 4.8, Mode 3). Third, these different models of organising relations are able to coexist in the same space

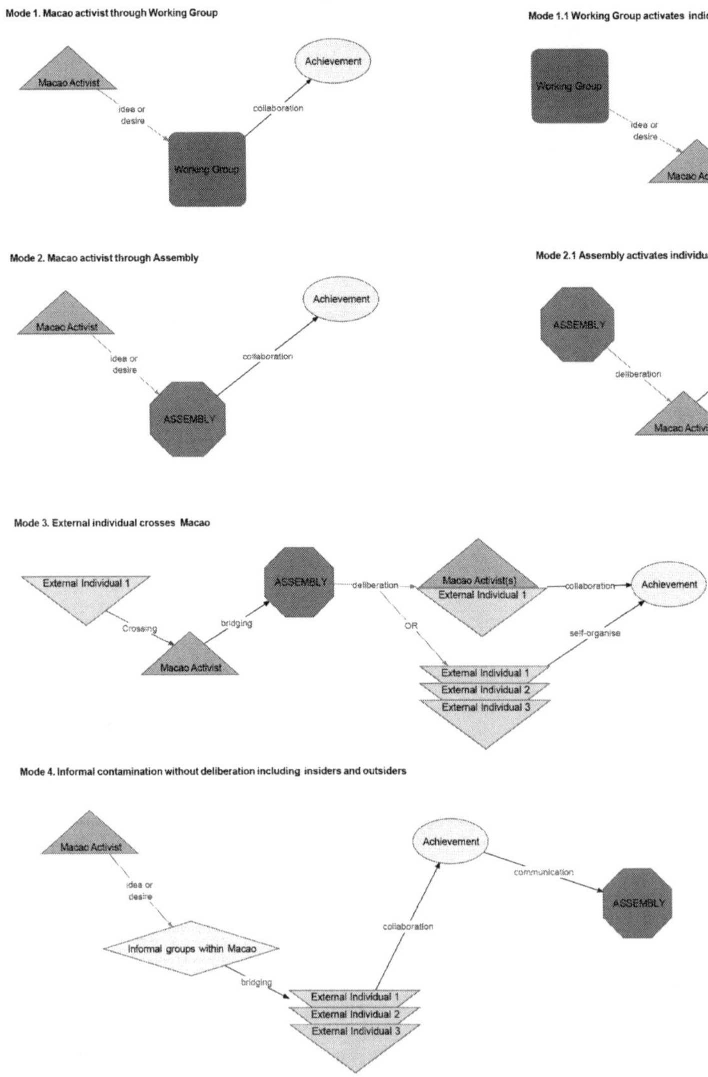


**Figure 4.8 Macao's Social Mechanics**. *Source*: Created by author.

because of a *desired instability*, which – paradoxically – constitutes a 'sound floor' on which activities are based. Instability is a feature that characterises many organisations nowadays, both within and outside the realm of social movements, and it does not represent an unintended negative outcome of systemic dysfunctions. As Chiappello and Boltanski (2005) have highlighted, capitalism itself has drawn ideas from countercultures and implemented them in new management theories. In Macao's case, however, there has been a step forward as there is a shared awareness of being already subsumed into the neoliberal capitalist mode of production, the reflexive desire to have an unstable organisation represents the outcome of a process of political subjectification in which the refusal of work (Lazzarato 2014) appears as a key component. Rather than being a hegemonic – and thus naturalised and pre-reflexive – frame for Macao, the desire to be unstable constitutes a safeguard from self-exploitation.

The second finding deals with the organisation of participation along with the opposed and coexisting notions of horizontality and hierarchy. In Macao, there is a constantly shifting equilibrium of radical inclusion and leadership. On the one hand, radical inclusion is granted by the 'crossings' by other subjects and groups that Macao, as a process and as a space, empirically supports by having, for instance, a weekly assembly that is fully open. Regardless of their status – individual, group, acting inside or outside Macao – everyone in these assemblies is welcome and is granted a space in which it is possible to propose ideas and collaborations. However, this does not necessarily imply agreeing dogmatically with horizontality. In fact, leadership, and not leaders, represents a concrete reality in the activities of Macao, as has been substantiated in the second case study. As Simon Western (2014) has suggested, leadership in many contemporary movements is not de facto, already in place, it is an unavoidable and beneficial feature of every human grouping, as anarchists have also acknowledged. In Western account, an unwillingness to recognise leadership in movements like Occupy and Indignados caused growing dissatisfaction among activists and led to their dissolution. What is different in Macao, then? As I have stressed previously, desire[17] is actively pursued and given free rein so that it can permeate assemblies or, in other cases, simply ignore them and bypass them. Furthermore, there is a strong recognition of individual qualities and differences. Different forms of leadership are simultaneously co-present as they are disseminated in the social body of Macao, leading projects that might involve highly diverse skills and interests (e.g. organising a theatre festival vs. a seminar on free software).

The third and main finding relates to the overall organisational model of Macao. In chapter 3, I highlighted how the event represents a fundamental logic that guides Macao activists' political action in the public sphere. I have also stressed how it contains a deep ambivalence, especially to the extent that the threshold separating a staged event from a disruptive event, a media event from a more authentic event that is bodily and emotionally perceived, is very thin. This ambivalence is still present and the event seems to play a role in the mechanics that govern the organisation of Macao. From this point of view, the event is the minimal unit which compels activists to cooperate within a just-in-time regime of production that appears all too close to the regimes experienced by less politicised cultural workers. Within a framework that is characterised by a desiring and desired instability, however, events offer a manageability that leaves room for a critique of work beyond self-exploitation, as highlighted by the slow work rate that defines many of Macao's activities (see Case Study 1 in Box 4.1). Furthermore, what must be considered is the fact that the current Italian political arena[18] is not capable of mediating the needs originating from art and cultural workers, as traditional collective actors appear unfit and unwilling to represent them, thus leaving a gap to be filled.

Such a gap has been occupied by hybrid organisations that bear the heritage of social movements, artistic avant-gardes and workers' movements, like Macao and many others around Italy and Europe. If, traditionally, action was structured around organisations producing events (e.g. trade unions calling for a general strike or a rally), if the main economic system is centred around the event economy, if access to power through institutionalisation (e.g. becoming a union) or co-optation is not either feasible or desirable anymore, if the only means available to change capitalism are from within (since there is no outside), what happens to the concept of organisation for this type of hybrid movement? In this context, as highlighted by the experience of Macao, the appropriation of a capitalist logic for political purposes requires us to rethink organisation as we are used to conceive of it (i.e. an organisation that produces events) and rather to think of it as a linking of events. In other words, as the event becomes a key organisational device, the new organisation is not a unity that produces events to persist with its structures and roles, but becomes a series of events that loosely interweave the organisation of action and production.

# Chapter 5

# Producing Culture in the Neoliberal City

This chapter explores activism among cultural operators in urban social movements (Mayer 2009), focusing in particular on their capacity to produce an alternative cultural model to that of the *creative city*. Their constant struggle regarding the redefinition of what our society should look like. Due to the decline of manufacturing-based production as the engine of urban development, culture and creativity have become a common means of promoting urban economy and growth. Instead of promoting bottom-up individual creativity, creating the conditions for a more democratic and open culture, or supporting cultural social innovation (André, Brito Enriques and Malheiros 2009; Chatterton 2000; Colbert 2011; d'Ovidio and Pradel 2013; Peck 2005; Pratt 2011; Vicari Haddock 2010; Vivant 2013), urban governments have implemented neoliberal cultural policies oriented towards using culture to revitalise and to promote the city in the global arena.

Notwithstanding the harsh criticism that has emerged within the academic world, neoliberal cultural policies have largely been put into practice in most European and U.S. cities; yet, after ten years, the creative city model has betrayed its promises. Creative and cultural operators often do not recognise themselves in the policies proposed in their name. As an alternative, avant-garde culture is still at the margins, the production and promotion of culture is mainly directed to the middle class, and a large segment of creative labour is living in precarious and insecure conditions (Harvey 2012; McLean 2014; Novy and Colomb 2013). As McRobbie claims, 'the creative sector finds itself full of young people who are burnt out, exhausted, unable to consider having children, and often self-exploiting on the basis of the "pleasure in work" factor' (2011, 33).

Cities are increasingly transformed by immaterial economy, new patterns of consumption and gentrification (Zukin 1991, 1995).[1] Arts and culture, in general, have been systematically used in order to revamp the urban environment and to promote neighbourhood development into new marketable places, where the art scene has been exploited by economic forces (Bonet, Colbert and Courchesne 2011; Kirchberg and Kagan 2013; Lloyd 2006). Nevertheless, the promotion of urban growth through culture is achieved with high social costs: there are conflicts among populations, and with an increase in the value of real estate comes the displacement of artists and disadvantaged people (Zukin 1989). Public spaces are affected by a particular kind of cultural colonisation that is obtained through forms of urban marketing and consumption, and that leads to a gradual loss of the publicness of public spaces themselves.

Regarding the complex relation between capital and the cultural or art sphere, Harvey recognises that 'the problem for capital is to find ways to co-opt, subsume, commodify and monetize such cultural differences just enough to be able to appropriate monopoly rents there from' (Harvey 2012, 110). Harvey makes a step forward and has hypothesised that the more neoliberal cities exploit art and culture, the more people involved in art and culture themselves tend to oppose such an instrumentalisation: 'The widespread though usually fragmented struggles that exist between capitalistic appropriation and past and present cultural creativity can lead a segment of the community concerned with cultural matters to side with a politics opposed to multinational capitalism' (Ibid., 111).

Criticisms and political resistance are rather common within the art sphere (Borén and Young 2013; Kirchberg and Kagan 2013); however, they have also recently emerged within the larger realm of the cultural industries (see Grodach and Silver 2012, for numerous examples). It is not only artists who are now involved in opposing the neoliberal city – opponents also include those people to whom neoliberal urban policies are directed. This 'creative class' is aware of the politics of the exploitation of culture (Peck 2005) and refuses most of the actions that are formulated in its name (Novy and Colomb 2013). These kinds of protest often reach a larger scale and can be recognised as urban social movements: starting from small-scale issues or much more narrowly focused aims, they tend to enlarge and address larger issues linked to urban politics more generally, and they look for support from other social movements in the city (Mayer 2009; Pradel and Martì-Costa 2012). The NiON (Not in Our Name) movement represents a clear example: it is a collective of creative professionals and activists, which, in November 2009, published a manifesto entitled 'Not in Our Name' denouncing the use and instrumentalisation of arts, culture and creativity in urban policies in Hamburg, Germany (Novy and Colomb 2013).

## ALTERNATIVE FORCES AS CULTURAL PRODUCERS IN THE CREATIVE CITY

Cities are often addressed as privileged sites for arts and culture, as, on the one hand, they promote and organise culture production and consumption, and, on the other, they accommodate some elements of structural instability that can nourish the local creative atmosphere. As Bertacchini and Santagata claim, elements of revolution are important for the creative atmosphere of a given place. Moreover, the actors in such transformations are often groups that present themselves as extraneous to the local history and context (Bertacchini and Santagata 2012).

Alternative, underground culture has a strong role in feeding the creative industries, and close links are built between mainstream knowledge (re)production and underground creativity (Krätke 2012; Leslie and Rantisi 2011; Niessen 2009; Pruijt 2004; Vivant 2009). Vivant (2009), for instance, uses a semantic pattern that opposes the 'off' culture to the 'in' one. While the 'in' is organised and planned, the 'off' is often said to be spontaneous and opportunist; it is free of any constraints, and so becomes extremely creative and innovative. In the case of the theatre festival in Avignon Vivant shows how, little by little, the 'off' becomes the real festival: the place to show and to be, the real engine of the festival that attracts more people and more artists until a new 'of alternative appears'.

Pruijt, in his examination of squatting activities in Amsterdam, maintains that policymakers tend to recognise the squatting artists' workspaces as venues for cultural activities, and therefore as extremely valuable elements for the city. This leads to connections between the squatter scene and the local administration (Pruijt 2013). The Municipality of Amsterdam invested more than €40 million in the Breeding Places Amsterdam (BPA) project in 1999 (Pruijt 2004; Uitermark 2004), aimed at sustaining local cultural production with space and workshop provision.

Within the neoliberal European city, the alternative, underground, subcultural culture represents a scene that renders the urban space as attractive, not only for urban tourists and city users but also, and more importantly, for investors in urban regeneration programmes. Cultural milieus represent an asset, both in general cultural terms (for marketing, attracting tourists) and especially in terms of real estate and urban development, as 'they are charged with cultural capital which in the scheme of creative city policy becomes transformed by investors into economic capital' (Mayer 2013, 4). Cultural scenes, emerging from alternative or underground culture, are exploited as a branding asset that shows how cool and authentic (Zukin 2009) the city is. Therefore,

> neo-liberal urban policies on the one hand manage to incorporate alternative and subcultural activism including the creativity of squatters (who, in the process,

> may find it difficult to maintain their political autonomy), while on the other they entail intensifying repressive strategies, stricter laws, tougher policing, and hence more evictions and fiercer criminalization of squatting. (Mayer 2013, 5)

Paradoxically, even the activities of the most alternative and antagonistic cultural fringes end up contributing to gentrification of neighbourhoods, as cultural policy overlaps more and more with programmes of urban regeneration (Pratt 2011).

## POLITICAL MOBILISATION

Taking as its frame the idea of activism against the creative city model, here I analyse Macao's political mobilisation by cultural workers in Milan, Italy. A mobilisation opposed to local cultural policies. To what extent does Macao represent a real alternative to the neoliberal articulation of the creative city in Milan? To answer this question necessitates evaluating Macao's role in the cultural milieu at different levels (local, national, international) and requires that I ask another question: whether Macao is a political actor that is able to influence local cultural policy, and to what extent Macao is included in the urban governance of Milan. I must also consider Macao's claims and expectancies, and its possible process of normalisation.

## MILAN'S CULTURAL STRATEGIES

A long ethnography with in-depth interviews was conducted from May 2012 onwards, and a questionnaire was circulated to Macao activists as part of a 2014 survey. I collected fifteen answers from thirty key members of the organisation. Questions in the questionnaire were mostly open and related to Macao's capacity to promote culture in the city of Milan. Milanese cultural policy follows the neoliberal model based on city-consumerism and branding. It focuses on large and mass-participation events, to attract many people into town, which is not really aimed at promoting young or emerging artists, or even at looking at avant-garde production. This is even more remarkable because, during the 1950s and 1960s, the city hosted one of the largest artistic communities in Europe, with artists such as Manzoni or Fontana, or Burri, representing the peak of international art in that period. Cultural policies have been criticised for being elitists and event-centred (Alfieri 2009), supporting domesticated and mainstream proposals with the aim of producing big popular events.

The adoption of a narrative linked to creativity in Milan was also one of the causes of the sterilisation of most cultural realities based on heterogeneity and diversity, as shown by the eviction of most of the so-called *Centri Sociali*

(Squatting Europe Kollective 2013). In Italy *Centri Sociali* (autonomous cultural squatted centres) developed around the end of the 1970s, as a manifestation of radical left movements. In Milan during the 1980s, *Centri Sociali* experienced a great expansion, exactly in the period in which the Municipality was implementing a set of urban policies that were designed to build an image of the city based on luxury, and the design and fashion industry. By the 1990s, *Centri Sociali* became a real breeding ground for young, productive and talented workers, providing urban workshops for experimental creative professions in music, cinema, the web, software, interactive design and so on. Such places even became popular touristic attractions for young people passing through Milan. All the cultural and creative production that resulted from these places was opposed to the normalised branding of Milan, and often cultural production was a tool which was used to carry out political action (Gill and Pratt 2008). Today, such places have been either removed or normalised, because they have not been able to adapt to the new city's brand ideals. Many protagonists of that scene became successful creative professionals (often co-opted by the economic forces they were fighting against) – mainly abroad, since as a large part this 'creative class' of yesteryear had been pushed away from Milan.

In general, the Milanese cultural system is often accused of being close-minded and incapable of valorising local resources: 'almost everything in art is private, self-organized' (Fucking Good Art 2012, 25). Artists and commentators criticise the lack of institutional funds for the art sphere, which forces artists to respond to market logic and limits experimentation and the avant-garde (Agosti 2010). The city of Milan holds a large and valuable artistic heritage, such as private galleries, exhibition centres and independent associations, while many projects in the city aimed at connecting them in a cultural system have always failed.

The present Municipal Council was elected in spring 2012, and, as a progressive coalition among left-wing parties, it represents a strong break with the former right-wing governments that had led the city for many decades. Generally speaking, the new Council claims to adopt a more democratic and pluralist governance structure, one that is receptive to civil society and to bottom-up initiatives. Nevertheless, an assessment of this political strategy is difficult at the moment, as very few researchers have published analyses of it (see, for instance, Angelucci, Barberis and Kazepov 2014).

## IS MACAO AN ALTERNATIVE ANSWER TO THE 'CREATIVE CITY'?

Macao was born during the winter of 2011/12, as a part of *Lavoratori dell'Arte* (art workers), a group of artists, art critics, curators, journalists and activists who had been politically active in Milan since the previous autumn. Macao defines itself as the New Centre for Arts, Culture and Research of Milan. In the first phase of its existence, it was an idea in the making that became visible in April 2012, in the form of a Twitter profile, a YouTube channel and a Tumblr site.[2] Macao only became an open space for citizens to experiment with new modalities of art, culture and research in May 2012, when hundreds of cultural workers occupied an empty skyscraper (Galfa Tower) in the centre of Milan. They were evicted some days after the occupation, and a few weeks later, they managed to occupy the Exchange and moved there.[3]

## MACAO WITHIN THE POLITICAL ARENA

Does Macao constitute an answer to the neoliberal articulation of Milan's cultural policies? Is it an example of an open, bottom-up, innovative culture? Is it included in urban governance, such that it can influence local cultural policies? In order to answer these questions, it is necessary to trace Macao's genealogy. If we look at the past, we can consider Macao as a peculiar combination of distinct histories of Italian mobilisation.

The first historical period, more strictly political, relates to the wide field of the Italian radical left movement that is also linked to the experiences of the *Centri Sociali* as previously described. Since the early 2000s, this movement was particularly active around the themes of *precarity* (Neilson and Rossiter 2008), developing innovative political actions, combining an autonomist political culture with a highly creative and innovative repertoire of action (Mattoni 2012).

The second historical trend that led to the development of Macao is connected to mobilisations in which artists were directly involved. Pivotal to this respect are the struggles against gentrification brought about in Isola a formerly working-class neighbourhood in Milan, which underwent a strong and harsh process of de-industrialisation and gentrification. The artistic mobilisation (many participants who are also part of the Macao movement) denounced the interests of speculators, building a particular artistic narration called *fight-specific* involving many inhabitants of the Isola neighbourhood.

Finally, a third important connection in the history of Macao is the recent network of activists in Italy. In 2008–2009, a movement emerged among Italian art workers that denounced the scarcity of public funds for the arts and the precariousness of jobs within the cultural economy. In 2011, this movement organised the Italian National Network of Occupied Theatres[4] which was established after a large and very successful occupation in Rome in April 2011, where activists also aimed to give another cultural life to those spaces (see also Giorgi 2014).

Macao presents itself as a reality,[5] whose main constituency is composed of culture and knowledge workers. Macao's activists are not the usual squatters or typical political activists. They are, on average, thirty-four years old; they hold a university degree and work under precarious contracts in the artistic or knowledge sector. Notwithstanding their presence in the labour market (as their jobs are precarious), on average people devoted around thirty-three hours a week to the project and Macao's activists are often involved in more than one activity.[6]

Looking specifically at the governance of the Milanese cultural sector and the influence of Macao on local cultural policies, we can see that, in the early days of the Galfa Tower occupation, the Milanese Municipality adopted a strategy of recognition and normalisation at the same time. Indeed Macao was offered the use of an extensive space, owned by the Municipality, on the condition that Macao became a formal association. The interest shown by the Municipality was mainly due to the success of the occupation and the partial overlapping of the demands raised by Macao with the city council's political programme. At any rate, if the local government recognised Macao, it also aimed to normalise it. Macao rejected the proposal, claiming instead the right of spontaneous groups of citizens to self-govern the urban commons, outside of the framework of any top-down legitimisation. Later, Macao refused the Municipality's offer because it did not want to be opposed to, and be ostracised by, the numerous cultural associations of the city that, for many years, have been claiming space from the Municipality.

A second phase started when, in June 2012, Macao activists occupied the Exchange, shortly after their eviction from the Galfa Tower.[7] The building, a perfect example of Art Nouveau in Milan, is publicly owned and is located in a semi-peripheral area of the city. Despite their formally illegal status, the local government silently tolerates Macao's presence, allowing Macao to find resources to undertake cultural and artistic production. This relationship suits the local governance for two reasons. One is the fact that a left-wing-led administration is running the city, and second, it draws on a long tradition of the toleration of self-organised squats.[8]

Finally, in the early summer of 2014, a new phase began. The Municipality established a negotiating table in order to deal with abandoned spaces owned by the Municipality that could be used for social purposes. The aim of the negotiating table is to find ways to include informal associations or autonomous realities or collectives in the decisional process on the urban commons. Indeed, despite the numerous evictions in the 1990s and early 2000s, there are still a number of squatted places in Milan. Some of these are part of the cultural and political history of the city; some have been occupied for only a few years or even months. Nevertheless, the Municipality, with the aim of acknowledging both the lack of public space for cultural and political activities in the city and the cultural value of such movements, invited all the squatting realities in the city to the negotiating table, together with formal and institutionalised associations. Most of the autonomous organisations refused to negotiate. Only a few, including Macao, accepted. The ones who refused to negotiate intended this to be an action to signal their difference, as no compromises should be made with administrations that want to legitimise, but at the same time normalise such organisations. This normalisation was seen as a threat to the alternative character of these squats or social centres compared to the already existing more institutional agencies of the third sector, NGOs, and so on.

The attention given by the Municipality to the emerging bottom-up forces that shape the city is the outcome of a long process of valuing the commons that has been taking place in Italy since the early 2000s. This process has included a national debate (and referendum) about the privatisation of the water supply, and important discussions about public spaces in many Italian cities. Within the Milanese context, Macao members have been involved in this debate since its beginning and they have been very keen to raise such issues explicitly in the negotiations.

This negotiating table constitutes a major shift in the city's governance – at least in its founding premises, if not in its results (which are still undefined). It does not simply constitute an attempt to negotiate formally with squatters; it is a way to include grassroots organisations directly in urban policymaking. Moreover, Macao was able to ensure that the table adopted the *istruttoria pubblica* (public enquiry) legislative tool: through which citizens can directly contribute, express their stances and, with the support of municipal lawyers, transform them into a draft law that the city council is expected to discuss and vote upon. At this negotiating table, Macao's goal was first that of being recognised as an autonomous and not-institutionalised subject able, nonetheless, to be legitimised in the public arena. Second, the use of the space is at stake at the negotiation table. If the first aim has already been reached (recognition), as the table has been set, the second objective (to raise issues) is still very far from being achieved, as the negotiation is still going on.

## MACAO WITHIN THE CREATIVE MILIEU

The second dimension of our analysis concerns Macao's cultural offering. This is part of our attempt to understand if, and to what extent, Macao constitutes an effective answer to the creative city in terms of cultural production. In almost three years of activity, Macao has organised or hosted hundreds of events, including live events (music, performing arts), exhibitions, talks and cultural/artistic festivals. This demonstrates the know-how possessed by

Macao activists in terms of event organisation, and it makes clear the need for such a space in Milan. Macao's events vary considerably in qualitative terms: one can find more experimental and avant-garde forms of art (e.g. poetry readings) together with music (e.g. a concert of a famous Italian folk singer) or cultural events (e.g. a talk by Richard Stallman) that are capable of gathering large crowds. Macao hosts events organised directly by itself, co-organised in partnership with other entities – institutions, associations, or single individuals – or directed and managed entirely by 'external' actors.[9] In addition, the public is involved to different degrees in the events, as they can be part of a more traditional audience or be more involved in workshops or even in the co-creation of performances. In the case of events organised by external actors, Macao acts as a curator and gives particular attention to guaranteeing not necessarily the artistic quality of the artwork, but the quality of the process. An example will help to clarify this: if an amateur painter wants to exhibit his/her pictures he/she would never be allowed to do so if the quality of the artworks is bad; but if an association of elderly people in the neighbourhood organises the exposition of recycled chairs, Macao helps them and hosts the event, because it shares the social aims of the event.

This wide spectrum of cultural offering has been, by itself, part of the political project of Macao since its inception. Activists often refer to the concept of *crossings*, which implies that the space of Macao must be open, so that it can be freely crossed, and activists deem themselves responsible for ensuring the space is open. Similarly, on the idea of *publics*, Macao criticises the city's cultural offering as being an event economy; instead, it calls for a redefinition of the role of citizens in cultural events, as a more active and involved public.

Therefore, when seeking to understand if and how Macao constitutes a space that is able to contribute to a more pluralistic urban cultural offering, we must acknowledge Macao's practice of including instances, desires and projects that otherwise would not find any space in the city. Reacting against the paradigm of the creative city, Macao's effort is to try to give visibility and legitimacy to 'other' forms of culture – and to *make* culture, also in terms of new organisational and productive processes.

To what extent are Macao members embedded in the artistic scene at different levels?[10] According to the answers of my survey, almost all of the respondents are knowledge and creative workers, some of them are pure artists, or define themselves as such. Nevertheless, few of them are able to sustain themselves with their artistic activities and, for the most part, they have at least two different jobs. Macao is for them a very precious environment, as it provides a necessary space, in the first instance, for the activists to channel their desires and creativity beyond the market and its logic. It is commonly the case that, among the diverse tasks each activist carries out, there is also some part that coincides with their profession, with their day job. Participating in Macao represents an opportunity not just to satisfy an ingenuous need to dance outside a proper theatre or to do video editing for a political cause rather than a corporation: it is about an affective and material investment that activists make in order to create an alternative model of cultural production. Asked to list the three most significant cultural or artistic projects in their careers, almost two-thirds of respondents stated that these took place within Macao, or were possible thanks to it. For instance, one interviewee stated: '[Macao] allowed me to realise my wishes that I organised autonomously', or, again, another one claims: '[I could do it only in Macao] because a person who is not an artist wouldn't have the opportunity to perform elsewhere.'

Nevertheless, Macao is also more than this: it provides the chance to cooperate with leading figures in the cultural sector, and it sustains their autonomous projects with inspirations, ideas and relations, as it represents a hub within the broader artistic system. Indeed, regarding Macao and activist inclusion in the national and international art circuits, my survey and ethnography exposes that some key members have had commitments in the art system, including in art academies, biennales and contemporary art museums in Italy (MACRO – MAXXI) and abroad (MACBA, MG Ljubljiana). Such commitments support, but also help to explain, the wider network built by Macao. Key members' participation in the wider cultural and artistic scene represents a very important resource in terms of networking for other less connected members. For instance: '[Macao has been crucial for my artistic career] because it eased the meetings with customers and people from the cultural word' or 'I got in touch with the acting company [. . .] thanks to their links with Macao'. In addition, the following answer is extremely evocative of the importance of Macao as an open window on the cultural scene:

> Without Macao, it would be difficult to collaborate with internationally known professionals and artists, as Luca Bigazzi (director of photography working with many important Italian directors) or the Jerzy Grotowski and Thomas Richards' Workcentre. It is exciting to work, although underpaid, with those people whose artworks I have studied in my schoolbooks. These are the reasons why we are happy about the investments in Macao.

Indeed, events organised in Macao are generally the outcome of the wide network (national and international) of which Macao activists are a part, and show that the centre is clearly recognised by the art system. Nevertheless, the relationship between Macao and the official contemporary art system in Milan (mainly private galleries) is controversial. On the one hand, the strong political commitment of the Macao activists and artists seems to be the reason for the failure of cooperative projects between Macao and a number of important Milanese art galleries. On the other hand, Macao, from its very beginning, has been engaging in fertile partnerships within the sub-field of contemporary art, which combines reflexivity, criticism and activism.

## CONCLUSIONS

The chapter has focused on Macao's mobilisation which aimed to offer a stage for a different, open, bottom-up culture in the city of Milan. Our starting point is that in Western cities urban policies aimed at creating a so-called *creative city* (a mix of cultural policies, city branding and urban renewal) align perfectly with the neoliberal urban model. Such policies build an entrepreneurial city, on sale on the international market to the global middle class and to multinational corporations.

Recently, cities have hosted a new wave of urban social movements that, explicitly or not, have fought against such articulations of cultural and urban policies. In this chapter, I have conceived Macao as operating under such a framework: Milan is not atypical as a creative-neoliberal city. Macao offers a case study for understanding if, to what extent and how, creative professionals, artists and activists not only oppose the creative city but also offer an alternative model to it.

Artists have often been at the forefront of struggles: situationists were involved in May 1968 where Futurists and the Russian avant-garde contributed to the shaping of deep political transformations. However, if we connect the experience of Macao that I have presented in this study with similar struggles – in Austria (Graz), France (*Intermittents*), the United Kingdom (Shake, Liberate Tate, Art Not Oil), Former West, 16 Beaver Street in New York, Occupy Wall Street (and in particular the Illuminator project), Egypt (Moisereen) – what emerges is an entirely new meaning for these artist-based social movements. In each case, they are not just antagonising the status quo, contrasting certain policies with other ones, or marginalising themselves: rather, they are making the change, in a literal and in a material sense. In other words, they are trying to replace the welfare state and the increasingly institutionalised third sector. They reclaim a 'right to the city', but not in a self-referential way. They want to invent new ways to produce art and culture, but the main principle guiding all of these processes is that this is not aimed at an artistic self-proclamation. Discourses about authorship circulate in these spaces, but what is at stake, in more general terms, is how to establish a fruitful dialectic between the individual and the collective.

I analysed Macao by asking two groups of questions: 'Is Macao involved in the governance of the cultural sector in Milan?' and 'Is it able to influence the local cultural agenda – is it an actor involved in the process of producing policies?' Later, I asked whether Macao is embedded within the art world, and how it relates to it. Simply put, the answer is yes, Macao has been explicitly mobilised against at least three outcomes of the neoliberal creative city from its early stages: against gentrification, the precariousness of the creative workforce and the event-logic of cultural offerings. Considering their political stances and requests, Macao has been capable of translating the event economy of a creative city into an instrument of critique, adopting a logic of action based on the power – as well as the ambiguities – of the events. Therefore, it is possible to argue that Macao has a political voice that is recognised at the local level. Macao, for instance, is sitting at a negotiating table with the Municipality to define the future of empty and squatted places in the city which has the potential to play a role in building a new creative city, that 'move[s] beyond the tourism, heritage and consumption focus of many initiatives and [that] embrace[s] the full cycle of culture-making that includes cultural production' (Pratt 2011, 129). While the outcome of such negotiations is unclear, Macao's participation shows that the Municipality recognises Macao as a partner to work with regarding the city's future.

I have explored the artistic voice of Macao within the local, Milanese, arena and within the international art world. Macao's cultural schedule is extremely heterogeneous as it hosts a variety of events that differ in terms of artistic quality. In short, Macao fulfils three main functions: it stages different kinds of artists, it represents a crucial node in the artistic international network and it offers a high-quality, avant-garde culture that would not be exposed in Milan otherwise. Accordingly, at least in its practices, Macao represents a different option to the neoliberal articulation of the creative city, and it does so straddling the political arena and in the artistic world. Many issues remain open, however, among which I would like to emphasise one question concerned with the embeddedness of Macao in the political and the economic sphere: how can Macao go beyond its squatting and illegal nature, without losing its political character? Here the important issues of normalisation, institutionalisation and co-optation of Macao by both the Municipality and the market arise.

Macao is certainly not devoid of contradictions. Its fight against gentrification might well result in gentrification of the area it is trying to protect, and its cultural production models might coincide with processes of self-exploitation, with similar contradictions to those evident in vast sectors of social entrepreneurship and of the collaborative economy. In Macao, activists are conscious of such risks, but nevertheless they have decided to take the risk and have made the political choice of taking action. Furthermore, they intend to cope with these risks in different ways: for instance, to deal with self-exploitation they discuss and experiment with forms of economic redistribution inspired by mutualistic ideas. What has yet to be established is if such models can be further developed into a sustainable alternative to the creative city.

## *Chapter 6*

# Doing the Unthinkable

## *Becoming Institutions*

This book has demonstrated how art plays a role in processes of political mobilisation by drawing on ethnographic research that combines interviews, digital methods and questionnaires. I have also demonstrated how art's role in social movements cannot and should not be reduced to an instrumental or expressive one. Examining the role played by art in an artist-led mobilisation like Macao made it possible to understand how art nurtures and stimulates the different fields of activity and phases of a social movement.

In chapter 1, I highlighted how social movements have increasingly embodied a progressive approach, highlighting the evolution of social movement practices in this direction and the parallel adoption of deliberative theories by social movements. I have also pointed out how the emerging wave of artist mobilisations differs from social movements and how a micro-sociological cultural approach to the study of social movements is ideally suited to render meaning-making processes connected to social movements in depth. Notwithstanding the relevance of art in contentious practices, very few studies have covered the inter-linkages between art and political mobilisation, especially in the debate around social movements. This work is intended to contribute to this emerging field.

In chapter 2, I presented the ethnographical approach adopted in the research. In particular, I focused on my position as a researcher in the field. As the literature has highlighted, in order to render social movement research more dynamic, a single-sited ethnography is not only the most suitable method for capturing complexity, but it also constitutes a remedy for the routinisation of research on social movements, which has usually been too focused on comparative studies or quantitative analysis. However, considering the peculiarity of my position in the field, for my qualitative research to be accountable it was necessary for it to be reflexive and take a long time frame. Finally, I explained how digital methods have proved to be crucial in allowing a native take on the digital environment in which actors were acting and I showed the fruitful interplay between traditional ethnographic research methods and digital methods.

In chapter 3, I delineated Macao's mobilisation from its early theoretical beginnings, through its occupation of Galfa Tower and its subsequent home, the Exchange. Art, in the first, and most intense, phase of Macao's mobilisation, led me to reconsider the explanatory power of connective logic theories. Triangulating digital methods with ethnographic insight, I established how theorisation about social movements' logics of mobilisation should take into account the emotions and the planning that precedes the aggregation produced by social media. In fact, by adopting a pragmatic approach – that is, focusing on the contextual meaning-making produced by actors in their situated interactions – I outlined the limits of a paradigmatic/classical approach that privileges the concept of a highly individualised actor, neglecting the dimensions of collective identity-building. In this way, we are able to understand the role of artists in the planning and development of Macao as being a fundamental source of the so-called stitching mechanisms. Thus, the logic of Macao's mobilisation is eventful – stressing the role of artists in reworking the event economy that is the basis of the economic and social life (in neoliberal terms) in Milan. Through Macao, the event becomes a disruptive device that is capable of intercepting the desire and the need of a substantial part of Milanese citizenry. One that is capable, at the same time, to grant a radical openness to the project of becoming Macao.

In chapter 4, I moved on to analyse the organisational aspects of Macao, combining ethnographic insights with digital data. By focusing on the phase in which Macao's activities and its constituency were stabilised, I was able to stress how relations became a key site of development for the movement. This finding of the organisation of Macao corroborates the explanatory logic that was elaborated in the previous chapter. Macao's mobilisation confirms once more that mobilisations are born and endure as more than the result of drawing together atomised or monadic individuals thanks to an ephemeral social and political effervescence that is mediated by digital media. Rather, a core of members were capable of deploying an open organisational mechanic in which the becoming of Macao itself was the product of both individual and collective endeavours. By looking closely at mobilisations, we find that what appear to be crowds becoming affinity groups, working groups, friendships, and temporary alliances that are bound together by a shared experience and by a common desire. Whereas horizontality has become more than a feature of recent social movements – namely, something more similar to a normative discourse – leadership and hierarchy have become something to be avoided at all costs. My research contributes to the recent discussion in this respect where I argue that openness and radical inclusion coexist with recognised – multiple and temporary – leadership. Finally, in Macao, the event becomes a key organisational device. The new organisation is not a unity that produces events in order to persist with its structures and roles, but becomes a series of events that loosely interweave the organisation of action and production. This overall organisational form of Macao in response to external constraints and internal demands may indicate the form of future hybrid movements, in which political struggle and new forms of life and value-production coexist.

Chapter 5 evaluated Macao's struggles and to what extent Macao, and the global wave of art activism more generally, constitutes an alternative to the neoliberal articulation of the creative city in Milan. How it struggles. On the one hand, I asked whether Macao is a political actor that is able to influence local cultural policy and to what extent it is included in the urban governance of Milan. Related questions concern Macao's claims and expectations, and its possible process of normalisation. On the other hand, I evaluated Macao's role in the cultural milieu at different levels (local, national, international).

Having explored Macao's artistic voice, I found that it is based on an extremely heterogeneous cultural activity: event organisation. Macao hosts disparate kinds of events, both in their nature (performative, musical, cultural) and in terms of their artistic quality. Since, as I have explored in the previous chapter, individual desires and interests often result in the activation of links and experiences that could not be managed by a centralised body as an all-overseeing assembly. In considering Macao's cultural production, which is articulated through Macao's particular political and artistic voice, I can pin down three main functions: it stages different kinds of artists; it represents a crucial node in the artistic international network; and it offers a high-quality, avant-garde culture that would not otherwise be exposed in Milan. Therefore, I can conclude that Macao does represent a different option to the neoliberal articulation of the creative city; and it does so both in the political arena and in the artistic world.

Furthermore, analysing Macao's position towards urban governance, it is possible to argue that Macao has, indeed, a political voice that is recognised at the local level. Macao sits at a negotiating table together with the Municipality to define the future of empty and squatted places in the city. While the outcome of such negotiations is unclear, Macao's participation shows that the Municipality recognises Macao not as the squatted cultural centre, to be normalised or even evicted, but as a partner to work with regarding the future of the city.

These three core chapters (3, 4 and 5) – each adopting a different logic, different approaches and partially drawing on different bodies of academic literature – are proof of the complexity involved in studying recent mobilisations. The approach that I have adopted in this study aimed to make it possible to understand the relationship between art and mobilisation. However, during this process, I have realised that mobilisation is not just a protest, it embodies a number of fields and elements that have to be dealt with by an interdisciplinary approach. This is why, inspired by my findings, I decided to articulate my analysis of Macao by dividing it into three main areas: action, relation and production. Such an approach has been useful to understand Macao's mobilisation and, as I have argued, because it may be the only way to make sense of an emergent wave of hybrid political organisations.

Macao's mobilisation is clearly a part of the wider process that has recently taken place in the art world, and that has involved political artists in particular. Connected to a widespread crisis in the job market, with jobs that are increasingly unsatisfying, their endeavour is directed towards a construction of a new meaning for living. In this sense, it is also rather difficult to insulate their being artists who engage in mobilisation from their being workers trapped in the neoliberal mechanisms of just-in-time creativity. It is increasingly difficult to separate all of this from their simply being citizens, and ultimately human beings, in constant struggle regarding the redefinition of what our society should look like. It is even more difficult to separate them from what seems to be an emerging common front of struggle. A number of different groups, ranging from neo-ruralism, peer-to-peer cooperation and decentralised currencies show interesting overlapping political sensitivities (Bollier and Conaty 2014).

As I have tried to highlight in the previous chapters, processes of political subjectification seem to play an important role in the critical appropriation of different heritages and present moments: the heritage of antagonism, of self-governing, of direct action; the present moment of networks, crowds and collaborative practices. The appropriations of such devices are again the process of connecting individual competences and desires in a politically driven collective process.

Most importantly, artists want to do all this, without ceasing to be artists. But what does it mean for these art-activists to be artists today? Being an artist means to serve a greater goal, to put forward the idea that precarity can be overcome with joy and the beauty of being together. I think this is the deepest and most defining thing I have found in Macao and in the other spaces I have visited. This finding might not seem to represent a sound sociological argument, but the kindness and the care for each other I have seen demonstrated by the artist-activists in these spaces is not common. Conflicts arise, but they are handled with the care of a soul that has cultivated other perspectives about how to interact with others. In this sense, the contribution of artists to the global struggle lies in bringing forth an alternative, by making that alternative a reality, without wasting energy on conflicts that are already lost because they are fought in a deeply asymmetrical field. In this sense, I see the contribution of artists to the struggle, even in Milan alone, in the interaction with other urban movements, as being capable of producing a whole new field in which to conduct the struggle.

This is akin to the notion of radical imagination conceived by Castoriadis (1987) as it stresses the relevance of the indeterminacy of our futures. Radical imagination departs from classical Marxist orthodoxy, stressing how, by virtue of our own capacity to imagine, we can envisage radical alternatives and, most importantly, take ownership of this radical openness. A position which echoes the openness unfolding from events as discussed in previous chapters, especially referring to the work of Maurizio Lazzarato. In this vein, we can find a common root in the fascination within movements for theories that loosely relate to the post-workerist canon. These include the theories of Spinoza, mostly mediated by the work of Althusser, Toni Negri and Gilles Deleuze. During my ethnography, I have often found many references to the thoughts of these authors, and this connects to the fundamentally alternative notion of politics that has been put forth by Spinoza and recuperated by Althusser and Negri. Following the genealogy of Spinoza offered by Renault and Sibertin-Blanc (2018) of 'left-wing Spinozism', Althusser refuses to grant individuals the autonomy of a sovereign subject, and therefore places conscience in an infinite chain of causal determinations. While Negri places his emphasis on the idea of multitude; a population that has not entered into a social contract with a sovereign political body, and such individuals retain the capacity for political self-determination. In both cases, it is about building a politics of power whose performative action is to envision subjects as an antithesis to power and an autonomy from established governmentalities. This resonates with the major transformations that are storming the ways in which we will produce and exchange ideas in digital futures. Decentralised architectures, including cryptocurrencies and blockchain technologies, self-governing of the commons, co-governing the city, living law and not codified law – these are all processes that share with the artistic mobilisation a post-dialectical frame.

To conclude this journey, based on my ethnography on Macao and its surroundings, my attempt is to pin down some of the functions that art has played in mobilisation: as an instrument, as a set of practices and as a frontier.

## ART AS AN INSTRUMENT

Although I have repeatedly called for a non-instrumental view of artistic practices in the process of political mobilisation, art has been used as a tool in this mobilisation. Even in times of severe budget cuts to arts and culture, particularly perceivable in Italy, art benefits from centuries of an alleged autonomy from power. This picture has been contested by recent developments in art criticism. In addition, a superficial investigation might produce evidence that the art world, its actors, institutions and economic models are anything but detached from the struggles that affect societies. Nonetheless, a residual aura has remained, even in a country like Italy in which a minister of culture claimed that budget funds for arts and culture had to be sacrificed because 'With art you cannot feed yourself'. Artists in the national mobilisation of what has been defined as the Network of Occupied Theatres exploited this residue to protect their struggle, to save historical spaces and to recuperate abandoned places. More than that, they shielded smaller movements, such as housing movements, whose bargaining capital with institutions was insufficient because their struggles were simply not visible. By unveiling the abandonment of historical spaces and whole areas of the city, the movement has gained considerable exposure, and through that exposure, it has secured important successes.

## ART AS A SET OF PRACTICES

Art is an immense repository of practices to convey symbolic meanings. Happenings, situations, performances, the figurative, the abstract, the visuals – artistic repertoire is practically unlimited, and it is constantly being reworked in light of new technical developments. Media art is one example of this, but in the case of Macao, it also means to produce an institutional communication that is capable of conveying meaning through form. In this sense, what appears particularly relevant is the coupling of a high capacity to decode the complexity of the present, but also the ability to produce signs that connect with people's experience. Consider, for instance, the path that Italian political art has taken since the 1970s: from the creative wing of the autonomist movement, through the underground culture of the 1980s, cyber culture and new punk, to relational and participatory art in the 1990s. Furthermore, the fundamental social and collective nature of artistic practices, coupled with the continuity with artisanship, created the ideal conditions for a fruitful and rich collaborative political endeavour.

## ART AS A FRONTIER

Recent debates on art (Whybrow 2011) highlight how we might have reached the point where everything, and yet nothing, might be art. Art has no defined boundaries, and art becomes practically impossible to define. In this process of the endless pushing of disciplinary boundaries, the most interesting development in respect of artistic political involvement is artists becoming researchers of contemporary society. Macao, in this respect, is probably the most advanced node of the Italian network: it experiments with cryptocurrencies and financial algorithms, and it engages directly with the most complex, yet compelling, challenges of our times. In fact, what these mobilisations show us is a continued effort in seeking alternative ways to co-govern our cities, reclaiming a right to determine the cultural production in a more autonomous way. Throughout this ethnography, we also saw how social movements have experimented with new avenues in the quest to make the livelihoods of artists and creatives more sustainable. In a constantly re-negotiated dialogue with the desires and the ambitions of their constituencies, autonomous art institutions have proved to be pivotal in showing empirically what alternatives can be crafted with their own work to serve political goals, that supports gendered struggles and a politics of difference, and an attempt to recast social hierarchies. Looking back at the myriad of initiatives that these institutions host, they are laboratories of inclusion that derive their relevance from the impact they are able to produce at the local level on several dimensions: providing a physical space for alternative ideas to be embodied; offering a discursive platform in which the horizon of utopia is momentarily opened up; delivering an economic platform that attempts and partially succeeds to sustain the lives of their members through direct and indirect means via a basic income and a way to accrue social capital thanks to the density of the ties these spaces are able to produce, and, in turn, attract even more ties – setting an example that has been included in pilot case studies in several EU-funded Research Projects as Commonfare and D-Cent.

I would like to conclude by looking towards the future, and in particular to *Global Activism: Art and Conflict in the 21st Century*, a 600-page volume curated by Peter Weibel (2015) which brings together a number of influential thinkers. One sentence that particularly caught my attention is: 'Activism may be the first new art form of the twenty-first century'.

# Notes

## INTRODUCTION

1. There is a well-documented history of these overlaps, some of which we have traced in the introduction of the book *ArtWORK: Art, Labour and Activism* that I curated with Paula Serafini and Jessica Holtaway (Serafini et al. 2017).

2. This historical interlocking between post-feudal renaissance and the current state of capitalism has been highlighted by Adam Arvidsson in his most recent book *Changemakers: The Industrious Future of the Digital Economy* (Arvidsson 2019).

## CHAPTER 1

1. In an international relations debate, realist and neo-realist scholars posit, to a varying extent, the crucial role of the state regarding monetary policy and national defence. See Helleiner (1995) and Kirchner (2007).

2. To understand the proportions of this crisis, it is relevant to cite the results of a survey ($n$ = 24,000) conducted by Gallup (2002 cited by Castells 2004), which reported that two-thirds of the world's population believes that their countries are not governed in accordance with their peoples' will.

3. I refer to the pre-eminence of financial operations within the capitalist paradigm, understood as a response of the owners of the means of production (as a class) to the reformist decades of the 1960s and the 1970s (Gallino 2011, 2012).

4. A United Nations Development Report 2011 (UN Development Programme (UNDP), 2011) shows a trend of decreasing Human Development Index (HDI) registered in all countries, regardless of their original level of HDI. Social inequalities and environmental threats are thus affecting highly developed countries such as South Korea (−17% in HDI) or the Czech Republic (−5%) and underdeveloped countries such as Sierra Leone (−42%) and Bangladesh (−27%). Also, the Organisation for

Economic Co-operation and Development (OECD) has released a report which confirms this negative trend (OECD, 2011).

5. For our purposes here, it would be reductive and misleading to refer to a commonly accepted notion of civil society to the extent that it implies a certain institutionalisation of movements and a liberal political philosophy which postulates a rigid distinction between the different realms of society. Thus, I refer here to 'civil society' as an umbrella term, and retain its normative implications.

6. Occupy and Indignados are two movements that emerged in 2011. The first arose in New York and spread to hundreds of U.S. cities and dozens of other countries. The second Spanish movement reclaimed 'real democracy' and had a lasting effect in the institutional arena as parts of the movement, for instance, created or joined Podemos, a Spanish political party. These movements emerged in the aftermath of the financial crisis of 2007 and are part of broader protests organised in the anti-austerity movement. They came to represent iconic examples of social movements that systematically exploited the new possibilities granted by social media for their political and cultural goals, in line with the precedents established by the Arab Spring (especially Tunisia and Egypt) and the Iranian 'Twitter' protests of 2009. Bennett does not define them as movements but, to signal a transition in the organisational form he prefers the term 'large-scale action networks' (Bennett and Segerberg 2012).

7. 'Occupiers! Stop Using Consensus!'. URL: http://occupywallst.org/article/occupiers-stop-using-consensus/ (consulted on April 2nd 2013).

8. Slavoj Žižek critically said Occupy Wall Street vision was impaired by the 'democratic illusion' for which 'the acceptance of democratic procedures as the sole framework for any possible change [. . .] blocks any radical transformation of capitalist relations' (Žižek 2012, 87).

9. For a cartography of the network, see the digital publication edited by Silvia Jop (2012) which collects self-narratives of the spaces involved. See also the book by Lidia Cirillo (2014) for a more recent collection of interviews with the main actors of the network.

10. My understanding of Habermas's discursive theory of the public sphere (1996) is that he does not advocate an illusory or idyllic dissolution of power. He rather seeks a more limited, although ambitious, linguistic fluidisation of power. For this particular point, I refer to the interpretation of Habermas's work made by one of his most prominent fellows in Italy, Walter Privetera (2001).

11. Although they are profoundly different, we can think of the interplay between Italian Fascism and Futurism, or the inspiration Situationism provided to the protests of 1968.

12. http://issuu.com/macaoMilan/docs/69300_ore

13. My translation of one of their claims. http://www.teatrovalleoccupato.it/chi-siamo

14. From the Macao journal. http://portale.macao.mi.it/script/diario.html

15. http://www.youtube.com/watch?v=kzHflu33ROg&feature=youtu.be

16. http://youtu.be/rr527Bduthc

17. If this new organisational pattern is due to technological developments, then there is a risk of endogeneity in positing that such platforms alter the core dynamics

of action in those connective logic movements born 'only' thanks to those digital platforms.

18. For the complex inter-linkages between these dimensions, privileging a work-centred point of view, see Menger (2001).

## CHAPTER 2

1. www.lavoroculturale.org.

2. Later on I realised that this restaurant was key to some internal dynamics, since a rather homogenous group had meals there before the weekly assembly every Tuesday at around 9.00 pm. This custom gave rise to complaints by other people regarding delays and disrespect for their own needs, and the relatively limited amount of time they could allocate to Macao due to family or job-related issues. Some colleagues in Macao were suspicious of these dinners, considering them as pre-assemblies, and complaining that, paradoxically, more was shared around that table than was shared in the assembly.

## CHAPTER 3

1. I am not implying that such an approach is not legitimate nor flawed. Semiotics, for example, a fundamental branch of cultural analysis, is almost entirely based on the analysis and decodification of 'texts' (in a wide sense) detached from their empirical conditions of production and reception, yet is a useful, precise field of analysis.

2. Here we intend a repertoire of action as a set of practices that are potentially infinite and empirically impossible to enumerate, and that are activated according to the specific circumstances that movements face and contribute to co-creating. On this, compare Mattoni's elaboration of the notion proposed by Charles Tilly (Mattoni 2012).

3. The issue is that creativity in protest often originates from subjects relatively deprived under certain capitals, while in my case study I am analysing highly trained artists with a high cultural capital. The question is relative to social position and professionalisation, so, in the first case, we would have a popular uprising in which creativity is a tool to use to attain more visibility, while in the second it is a disguised set of practices and sensibilities.

4. To explore their tactics further, see Holmes (2009).

5. A distinction is usually made between visual artists, performers and artists, as commonly understood, and workers, the 'maestranze' who are involved in the material aspects of arts. This division of labour is also evident in contemporary art (artists produce ideas and artisans specialise in metal or wood and craft artists in abstract ideas). This aspect is recognised by Macao's activists and is tackled through specific ideas and techniques that will be discussed more widely in chapter 4.

6. For Grégoire, such emancipatory horizons represent an array of demands imagined and developed collectively by social actors, whose ambition is to escape

subordination and promote institutions that are considered capable of advancing their collective conditions.

7. Problems have been identified concerning the efficacy of such a conceptualisation given that social movements, in their many different shapes, are always, first and foremost, a network (Diani 2013).

8. It is important to underscore that I have translated this from Italian and I was paid a remuneration for it. This is the result of the peculiar ethnographic relation established by me and Macao (see chapter 2) and of their ongoing work on the economic implications of their mobilisation (see chapter 5).

9. This is a delicate matter, because in one of the interviews (MI 2) it became clear how some people involved in the former LdA group experienced economic pressure, which was applied to encourage them to stop their critical activity.

10. According to Marco Baravalle (2009), one of the founders of *S.a.L.E. Docks* of Venice, a node of the Italian Network of Occupied Theatres, it took a decade-long effort to open up their causes to wider categories of workers.

11. I refer in particular to the numerous ruptures produced by Guy Debord within Situationist International in which the desire for purity was secondary to a wider inclusion (also see Perniola 1998).

12. The first video on YouTube shows a sketch of an Italian television programme that was popular during the 1980s, *Indietro Tutta*. The video refers to an imaginary commercial sponsor, called *cacao meravigliao*, a type of cocoa available in various versions the names of which are a parody of Brazilian words (*delicacao, spregiudicao* and *depressao*). In this first video, Macao changes the initial letter from 'c' to 'm' and recalls the fictional advertising of this imaginary product.

13. Bando is usually an announcement by public institutions (e.g. a local council might publish an open call for private companies to compete to provide ideas, projects or services) and in this case it was an open call put forth by Macao.

14. Until 8 May 2012, three days after the occupation, the main reference account for LdA was their Facebook page: https://www.facebook.com/lavoratoridellarte

15. I refer to the Autistici/Inventati group. In their manifesto they write: 'Our aim is to reclaim spaces on the internet where we can discuss and work on two levels: on the one hand, the right to and need for free communication, privacy, anonymity and access to digital resources; on the other, social projects linked to reality and struggles' http://www.autistici.org/en/who/manifesto.html [accessed 12/10/2014].

16. www.macaoMilan.org/comunicato_galfa.htm [accessed 12/10/2014].

17. http://bando.macao.mi.it/archive

18. www.lavoroculturale.org

19. Source: Official insights from Macao's Fan Page on Facebook, access to which was generously granted.

20. Source: Data gathered from Topsy (www.topsy.com).

21. Views updated to 20 August 2013.

22. Source: Elaboration of public data available on Macao's YouTube channel.

23. The concept of an event is deeply rooted in Western philosophy; however, especially since 1968 post-metaphysical philosophy reinvented the understanding of event. Badiou, Derrida, Deleuze, and Heidegger before them, were the

fundamental thinkers who attribute[d] in a relatively consistent manner the following features to the concept of an event: it is contingent, unpredictable, radically transformative.

## CHAPTER 4

1. It is telling what happened with *Occupare il conflitto* (occupying the conflict), a series of seminars created in response to episodes of sexist violence and homophobia that occurred within Macao. The idea embodied in this initiative was to publicly address relational dysfunctions within Macao: dysfunctions that also affected other collectives and, more generally, the 'outside' of Macao. http://www.macaoMilan.org/diario/fonte/occupare-il-conflitto

2. https://www.youtube.com/watch?v=N5dfNYVWe6Y

3. My translation. Link: https://www.youtube.com/watch?v=njqAiP4gX04 (Accessed December 2014).

4. See Berardi's analysis on contemporary society and suicides (Berardi 2015).

5. http://gephi.github.io/

6. The weight of an edge that connects each person (represented by a node) to the mailing list (small node at the centre of the graph) is based on the numbers of emails sent.

7. Brandes' (2001) algorithm is used to calculate betweenness centrality.

8. It must be noted these processes are key to the production of value and constitute a fundamental form of work in our digital lives (Arvidsson 2012), and a site of capitalist value-extraction (Terranova 2002).

9. A performance might as well integrate elements to make it shareable online, as we have hinted in the previous chapter considering the dual nature of the political events set in motion by Macao in actions and media events since their inception (see Macao's Media Practices).

10. Including different types of capital (social, cultural, symbolic) that are partially inherited and partially acquired through extensive education.

11. http://www.bloomberg.com/news/articles/2013-07-17/ligresti-family-members-arrested-in-fondiaria-sai-probe

12. http://www.macaoMilan.org/piazza_macao/diario/articoli/2013/07/19/nonemicalaluna-2/

13. http://www.macaoMilan.org/piazza_macao/diario/articoli/2013/07/19/nonemicalaluna-1/

14. See Financial Times article: http://www.ft.com/intl/cms/s/0/2025e524-51f7-11e3-8c42-00144feabdc0.html#axzz3f2terY29

15. https://www.youtube.com/watch?v=MuldQWuOQ5U

16. Crossing is a translation of the Italian word *attraversamento*, to pass through. In Macao's lexicon, the 'crossing' is a key concept representing their responsibility to leave Macao open to be permeated by third subjects as well as the enrichment deriving from it.

17. A fundamental keyword within Macao, it originates from the adoption of a Deleuzian and Spinozian frame.

18. In this respect the cases of Podemos in Spain and Syriza in Greece appear to be substantially different.

## CHAPTER 5

1. Immaterial economy refers to produced 'goods' associated with the creative industry or the knowledge economy.

2. Twitter: https://twitter.com/MacaoTwit; YouTube: https://www.youtube.com/user/wmacao; Tumblr: http://wmacao.tumblr.com/

3. For an accurate analysis of the subjectification of Macao as a political actor through the use of art see Valli 2015.

4. http://www.lavoroculturale.org/imprudenza/

5. The term reality is here used to differentiate Macao from other squatting movements (namely the *Centri Sociali*) that are usually called 'collectives'.

6. Data source: internal survey conducted by Macao itself, http://issuu.com/macaoMilan/docs/69300_ore

7. After Galfa Tower, Macao also occupied, and was immediately evicted from, an historical villa in the very centre of the city.

8. This is due to the need for a left-wing administration to signal a discontinuity with conservatives who governed the city for several mandates. The tolerance signals a progressive stance that places value on the capacity to perform (and display) an active listening on the needs that surge from the social fabric, including local communities and social movements.

9. For instance out of a total of 270 events in 2013, around 60 per cent were produced by Macao itself, while 40 per cent were co-organised with external actors.

10. Most of the information presented in this section derives from data collected via the questionnaires circulated in the summer of 2014.

# References


Agosti, G. (2010). *Le rovine di Milan*. Milan: Feltrinelli Editore.

Alexander, J. C. (2011). *Performative Revolution in Egypt: An Essay in Cultural Power*. New York: Bloomsbury Academic.

Alfieri, M. (2009). *La peste di Milan*. Milan: G. Feltrinelli.

Allegri, G. and Ciccarelli, R. (2013). *Il quinto stato*. Milan: Salani.

Alliez, E. and Osborne, P. (2013). *Spheres of Action: Art and Politics*. Cambridge, MA: MIT Press.

André, I., Brito Enriques, E. and Malheiros, J. (2009). 'Inclusive Places, Arts and Socially Creative Milieu'. *Social Innovation and Territorial Development*, pp. 149–166.

Angelucci, A., Barberis, E. and Kazepov, Y. (2014). *Governance Arrangements and Initiatives in Milan, Italy*. Urbino: DESP – University of Urbino Carlo Bo.

Arvidsson, A. (2006). *Brands: Meaning and Value in Media Culture*. London: Routledge.

Arvidsson, A. (2019). *Changemakers: The Industrious Future of the Digital Economy*. London: Polity.

Arvidsson, A., Caliandro A., Airoldi, M. and Barina S. (2015). 'Crowds and Value, Italian directioners on Twitter'. Forthcoming in *Information, Communication and Society*.

Arvidsson, A. and Peitersen, N. (2013). *The Ethical Economy: Rebuilding Value after Crisis*. New York: Columbia University Press.

Balasinski, J. and Mathieu, L. (2006). *Art et Contestation*. Rennes: Presses Universitaires de Rennes.

Balibar, E. (2011). *Citoyen sujet et autres essais d'anthropologie philosophique*. Paris: Puf.

Bandinelli, C. and Arvidsson, A. (2013). 'Brand Yourself a Changemaker!'. *Journal of Macromarketing*, 33(1), pp. 67–71.

Banfield, E. (1958). *The Moral Basis of a Backward Society*. New York: The Free Press.

Baravalle, M. (ed.) (2009). *L'arte della sovversione. Multiversity: pratiche artistiche contemporanee e attivismo politico*. Roma: Manifestolibri.
Barisione, M. (2009). 'Valence Image and the Standardisation of Democratic Political Leadership'. *Leadership*, 5(1), pp. 41–60.
Barker, C., Cox, L., Krinsky, J. and Gunvald, A. (eds.) (2013). *Marxism and Social Movements.* Leiden: Boston, Brill.
Basu, S. (1999). 'Dialogic Ethics and the Virtue of Humor". *Journal of Political Philosophy,* 7(4), pp. 16–35.
Beck, U. (1992). *Risk Society. Towards a Second Modernity*. London: Sage.
Beck, U. and Beck-Gernsheim, E. (2002). *Individualization: Institutionalized Individualism and its Social and Political Consequences*. London: Sage.
Becker, H. S. (1984). *Art Worlds.* Oakland: University of California Press.
Bedani F. and Ioannilli, F. (eds.) (2020). *Un cane in chiesa Militanza, categorie e conricerca di Romano Alquati.* Roma: DeriveApprodi.
Benford, R. and Snow, D. A. (2000). 'Framing Processes and Social Movements: An Overview and an Assessment'. *Annual Review of Sociology*, 26, pp. 611–639.
Bennett, W. L. and Segerberg, A. (2012). 'The Logic of Connective Action'. *Information, Communication and Society*, 15(5), 739–768.
Bennett, W. L. and Segerberg, A. (2013). *The Logic of Connective Action. Digital Media and the Personalization of Contentious Politics*. New York: Cambridge University Press.
Bennett, W. L., Segerberg, A. and Walker, S. (2014). 'Organization in the Crowd: Peer Production in Large-Scale Networked Protests'. *Information, Communication & Society*, 17(2), pp. 232–260. doi: 10.1080/1369118X.2013.870379
Berardi, F. (2015). *Heroes: Mass Murder and Suicide*. London: Verso.
Berger, P. L. and Luckmann, T. (1967). *The Social Construction of Reality: A Treatise in the Sociology of Knowledge*. London: Penguin Press.
Bertacchini, E. and Santagata, W. (2012). *Atmosfera creativa*. Bologna: Il Mulino.
Bimber, B., Flanagin, A. and Stohl, C. (2005). 'Reconceptualizing Collective Action in the Contemporary Media Environment'. *Communication Theory*, 15, pp. 389–413.
Bishop, C. (2012). *Artificial Hells: Participatory Art and the Politics of Spectatorship*. London: Verso.
Bollier, D. and Conaty, P. (2014). 'A New Alignment of Movements? A Report on a Commons Strategies Group Workshop'. Available online at: http://bollier.org/report-new-alignment-movements.
Bologna, S. and Banfi, D. (2011). *Vita da freelance. I lavoratori della conoscenza e il loro futuro*. Milan: Feltrinelli.
Bologna, S. and Fumagalli, A. (1997). *Il lavoro autonomo di seconda generazione: scenari del postfordismo in Italia*. Milan: Feltrinelli.
Boltanski, L. and Chiapello, E. (2000). 'Vers un renouveau de la critique sociale, an interview with Yann Moulier Boutang'. In *Multitudes*, 3. Available online at http://multitudes.samizdat.net/Vers-un-renouveau-de-la-critique.html.
Boltanski, L. and Chiapello, E. (2005). *The New Spirit of Capitalism*. London: Verso
Bonet, L., Colbert, F. and Courchesne, A. (2011). 'From Creative Nations to Creative Cities: An example of center-periphery dynamic in cultural policies'. *City, Culture and Society*, 2(1), pp. 3–8. doi: 16/j.ccs.2011.02.001.

Bonomi, A. (2008). *Milan ai tempi delle moltitudini. Vivere, lavorare, produrre nella città infinita*. Milan, Bruno Mondadori.

Borén, T. and Young, C. (2013). 'Getting Creative with the "Creative City"? Towards New Perspectives on Creativity in Urban Policy'. *International Journal of Urban and Regional Research*, 37(5), pp. 1799–1815. doi: 10.1111/j.1468-2427.2012.01132.x.

Bourdieu, P. (1996). *The Rules of Art: Genesis and Structure of the Literary Field*. Stanford: Stanford University Press.

Bourriaud, N. (2002). *Relational Aesthetics*. Dijon: Presses du réel.

Brandes, U. (2001). 'A Faster Algorithm for Betweenness Centrality'. *Journal of Mathematical Sociology*, 25(2), pp. 163–177.

Buchanan, D., Boddy, D. and McCalman, J. (1988). 'Getting In, getting On, getting Out, and Getting Back'. In A. Bryman (ed.), *Doing Research in Organizations*. London: Routledge.

Butler, J. (2011). 'Bodies in Alliance and the Politics of the Street'. *Transveral*, 9(2011). Available online: http://www.eipcp.net/transversal/1011/butler/en

Calhoun, C. (2001). 'Putting Emotions in Their Place'. In Goodwin et al. (eds.), *Passionate Politics: Emotions and Social Movements*. Chicago: University of Chicago Press, pp. 45–57.

Caliandro, A. (2014). 'Ethnography in Digital Spaces: Ethnography of Virtual Worlds, Netnography, and Digital Ethnography'. In P. Sunderland and R. Denny (eds.), *Handbook of Business Anthropology*. Walnut Creek: Left Coast Press.

Cammaerts, B. (2007). 'Jamming the Political: Beyond Counter-Hegemonic Practices'. In *Continuum: Journal of Media and Cultural Studies*, 21(1), pp. 71–90.

Care Collective. (2020). *Care Manifesto: The Politics of Interdependence*. London: Verso.

Carey, J. (1989). *Communication as Culture*. Boston MA, Unwin Hyman.

Carpentier, N. (2011). *Media and Participation: A Site of Ideological-Democratic Struggle*. Bristol: Intellect Books.

Cartocci, R. (2007). *Mappe del tesoro, Atlante del capitale sociale in Italia*. Bologna: il Mulino.

Castells, M. (2002). *Internet Galaxy: Reflections on the Internet, Business, Society*. Oxford: Oxford University Press.

Castells, M. (2004). *The Power of Identity* (2nd edition). Oxford: Blackwell.

Castells, M. (2009). *Communication Power*. Oxford: Oxford University Press.

Castells, M. (2012) *Networks of Outrage and Hope: Social Movements in the Internet Age*. Cambridge: Polity.

Castoriadis, C. (1987). *The Imaginary Institution of Society*. Cambridge: Polity Press.

CDEUM (2021). *Centro Studi Etnografia Digitable* [Centre for Digital Ethnography of the University of Milan]. Website. Italian. Available at: http://www.etnografia-digitale.it/ (Accessed 15 March 2021).

Chambers, S. (2003). 'Deliberative Democratic Theory'. *Annual Review of Political Science*, 6, pp. 307–326.

Chatterton, P. (2000). 'Will the Real Creative City Please Stand Up?' *City*, 4(3), pp. 390–397.

Ciccarelli R. and Allegri, G. (2011). *La Furia dei Cervelli*. Rome: Manifestolibri.

Cirillo, L. (2014). *Lotta di classe sul palcoscenico. I teatri occupati si raccontano.* Rome, Alegre.

Clemens, E. S. (2005). Two Kinds of Stuff: The Current Encounter of Social Movements and Organizations. In G. F. Davis, D. McAdam, W. R. Scott, M. N. Zald (eds.), *Social Movements and Organization Theory*. New York: Cambridge University Press, pp. 351–365.

Colbert, F. (2011). 'Cultural Policies and Creative Cities: Some Insights'. *City, Culture and Society*, 2(1). doi: 10.1016/j.ccs.2011.03.001.

Combes, H., Hmed C., Mathieu, L., Siméant, J. and Sommier, I. (2011). 'Observer les mobilisations': Retour sur les ficelles du métier de sociologue des mouvements sociaux' *Politix*, 2011/1 n° 93, p. 7–7. doi: 10.3917/pox.093.0007.

Corradi, C. (2013). 'Panzieri, Tronti, Negri: le diverse eredità dell'operaismo italiano'. In *Consecutio Temporum*», 5. Pubblicazione digitale: http://www.consecutio.org/2011/05/panzieri-tronti-negri-le-diverse-eredita-dell'operaismo-italiano/.

Corsani, A. (2009). 'Gli intermittenti dello spettacolo o la figura dell'eccezione francese. Breve storia di un'inchiesta in zona precaria'. In M. Baravalle (ed.), *L'arte della Sovversione. Multiversity: pratiche artistiche contemporanee e attivisimo politico*. Rome, Manifestolibri.

Couldry, N. (2012). *Media, Society, World*. Cambridge: Polity Press.

Crossley, N. and Roberts, J. M. (2004). (eds.). *After Habermas: New Perspectives on the Public Sphere*. Oxford: Blackwell.

Crouch, C. (2004). *Post-Democracy*. Cambridge: Polity Press.

Dalton, R. J. (2004). *Democratic Challenges: The Erosion of Political Support in Advanced Industrial Democracies*. Oxford: Oxford University Press.

Davis, G. F., McAdam, D., Scott, W. R. and Zald, M. N. (eds.) (2005). *Social Movements and Organization Theory*. New York: Cambridge University Press.

Dayan, D. (2005). Mothers, Midwives and Abortionists. Genealogy and obstetrics of Audiences and Publics. In Sonia Livingstone (ed.), *Audiences and Publics*. Bristol: Intellect Press

della Porta, D. (2005). 'Deliberation in Movement: Why and How to Study Deliberative Democracy and Social Movements'. *Acta Politica*, 40, pp. 336–350.

della Porta, D. (2008). 'Eventful Protest, Global Conflicts'. *Distinktion*, 17, pp. 27–56.

della Porta, D. (ed.) (2009). *Democracy in Social Movements*. London: Palgrave.

della Porta, D. (2011). *Democrazie*. Bologna: Mulino.

della Porta, D. and Diani, M. (2006). *Social Movements. An introduction* (2nd edition). Malden, MA: Blackwell.

della Porta, D. and Mattoni, A. (2012). Cultures of Participation and Social Movements. In A. Delwiche and J. J. Henderson (eds.), *The Participatory Cultures Handbook*. New York: Routledge, pp. 171–182.

Diani, M. (1992). 'The Concept of Social Movement'. *Sociological Review*, 40, pp. 1–25.

Diani, M. (2013). Oral presentation, European University Institute's Summer School on Political Mobilization, September 2013, Florence, Italy.

Di Martino, C. (2009). *Figure dell'evento. A partire da Jacques Derrida.* Milan: Guerini Scientifica.

d'Ovidio, M. and Pradel, M. (2013). 'Social Innovation and Institutionalization in the Cognitive–Cultural Economy: Two Contrasting Experiences from Southern Europe.' *Cities*. doi: 10.1016/j.cities.2012.07.002.

Dryzek, J. S. (2000). *Deliberative Democracy and Beyond.* New York: Oxford University Press.

Dryzek, J. S. (2009). 'Democratization as Deliberative Capacity Building'. *Comparative Political Studies*, 42(11), pp. 1379–1402.

Dumett, M. (2018). *Corporate Imaginations: Fluxus Strategies for Living*. Berkeley: University of California Press.

Exposito, Marcelo and Nuria Vila, dirs. (2007). *Tactical Frivolity*. PLACE: FILM COMPANY.

Eyerman, R. (2006). 'Towards a Meaningful Sociology of the Arts'. In R. Eyerman and L. McCormick (eds.), *Myth Meaning, and Performance: Towards a New Cultural Sociology of the Arts*. Boulder: Paradigm.

Eyerman, R. and Jamison, A. (1998). *Music and Social Movements,* Cambridge: Cambridge University Press.

Eyerman, R. and McCormick, L. (eds.) (2006). *Myth Meaning, and Performance: Towards a New Cultural Sociology of the Arts*. Boulder: Paradigm.

Fairclough, N. (1992). *Discourse and Social Change*. Cambridge: Polity Press.

Fine, G. A. (1979). 'Small Groups and Culture Creation: The Idioculture of Little League Baseball Teams'. *American Sociological Review*, 44(5), pp. 733–745.

Florida, R. L. (2002). *The Rise of the Creative Class: And How It's Transforming Work, Leisure, Community and Everyday Life*. New York: Basic Books.

Formenti, C. (2010). *Se questa è democrazia. Paradossi politico-culturali dell'era digitale*. Lecce: Manni.

Fraser, N. (1990). 'Rethinking the Public Sphere: A Contribution to the Critique of Actually Existing Democracy'. *Social Text*, 25/26, pp. 56–80.

Fraser, N. (1992). Rethinking the Public Sphere. In C. Calhoun (ed.), *Habermas and the Public Sphere*. Cambridge: MIT Press.

Freeman, J. (1972). 'The Tyranny of Structurelessness'. *Berkeley Journal of Sociology*, 17, pp. 151–164.

Fucking Good Art. (2012). *Art in the Age of Berlusconi. Viaggio in Italia 2011*. Roma, Rotterdam: Nero, Fucking Good Art.

Gallino, L. (2011). *Finanzcapitalismo. La civilità del denaro in crisi*. Turin: Einaudi.

Gallino, L. (2012). *La lotta di classe dopo la lotta di classe*. Rome-Bari: Laterza.

Gardiner, M. E. (2004). Wild Publics and Grotesque Symposiums: Habermas and Bahktin on Dialogue, Everyday Life and the Public Sphere. In N. Crossley and J. M. Roberts (eds.), *After Habermas: New Perspectives on the Public Sphere*. Oxford: Blackwell.

Gerbaudo, P. (2015). 'Rousing the Facebook Crowd: Social Media Campaigning, Digital Enthusiasm and the Online Plebeian Public Sphere in the 2011 Protest Wave'. Working paper presented at the University of Milan, 31st March 2015.

Giddens, A. (1987). *Social Theory and Modern Sociology*. Cambridge: Polity Press.

Gill, R. and Pratt, A. (2008). 'In the Social Factory? Immaterial Labour, Precariousness and Cultural Work'. *Theory, Culture and Society*, 25(7–8), pp. 1–30. doi: 10.1177/0263276408097794.

Giorgi, A. (2014). Le mobilitazioni dei lavoratori dell'arte e dello spettacolo. In L. Alteri and L. Raffini (eds.), *La Nuova Politica*. Napoli: EdiSes, pp. 110–135.

Goodwin, J., Jasper, J. M. and Polletta F. (2001). *Passionate Politics: Emotions and Social Movements*. Chicago: University of Chicago Press.

Gonzalez-Bailon, S. and N. Wang (2013). 'Networked Discontent: The Anatomy of Protest Campaigns in Social Media'. Forthcoming in Social Networks. doi: 10.2139/ssrn.2268165.

Graeber, D. (2008). *The Sadness of Post-Workerism, or "Art and Immaterial Labour" Conference: A Sort of Review*. Available online at https://libcom.org/library/sadness-post-workerism (Last accessed 30 June 2021).

Gray, M. and Caul, M. (2000). 'Declining Voter Turnout in Advanced Industrial Democracies', *Comparative Political Studies*, 33(9), pp. 1091–1122.

Graziano, V. and Trogal, K. (2019). 'Repair Matters'. *Ephemera: Theory and Politics in Organization*, 19(2), pp. 203–227.

Gregoire, M. (2013). *Les Intermittents du Spectacle*. Paris: La Dispute/Snédit.

Grodach, C. and Silver, D. (2012). *The Politics of Urban Cultural Policy: Global Perspectives*. London: Routledge.

Groys, B. (2014a). 'On Art Activism', *E-Flux*, 1/2014. Available online at: http://www.e-flux.com/journal/on-art-activism/

Groys, B. (2014b). *On the New*. London: Verso.

Habermas, J. (1996). *Between Facts and Norms: Contributions to a Discourse Theory of Law and Democracy*. Cambridge, MA: MIT Press.

Hammersley, M. and Atkinson, P. (2007). *Ethnography: Principles in Practice* (3rd edition). Taylor and Francis e-Library.

Harvey, D. (2012). *Rebel Cities: From the Right to the City to the Urban Revolution*. London: Verso.

Held, D. (2006). *Models of Democracy* (3rd edition.). Cambridge: Polity Press.

Helleiner, E. (1995). 'Explaining the Globalization of Financial Markets: Bringing States Back in'. *Review of International Political Economy*, 2(2), pp. 315–341.

Hess, C. and Ostrom, E. (2011). (eds.). *Understanding Knowledge as a Commons*. Cambridge, MA: MIT Press.

Hine, C. (2000). *Virtual Ethnography*. London: Sage.

Holmes, B. (2009). 'Marcelo Expósito's Entre Sueños: Towards the New Body.' *Revue du Crieur*, 17(10), pp. 100–114. Available at: https://marceloexposito.net/pdf/brianholmes_entresuenos_skor.pdf (Last accessed 15 June 2021).

Hutchby, I. (2001). 'Technologies, Texts and Affordances'. *Sociology*, 35(2), pp. 441–446.

Isola Art Center (2013). *Fight-Specific Isola. Arte, Architettura, Attivismo e il Futuro della Città*. Berlin: Archive Books.

Jasper, J. (2001). 'L'art de la Protestation Collective'. In D. Cefai and D. Trom (eds.), *Les formes de l'action collective*. Paris: Editions EHESS, pp. 135–159.

Joerges, C. and Neyer, J. (1997). 'From Intergovernmental Bargaining to Deliberative Political Processes. The Constitutionalization of Comitology'. *European Law Journal* 3, pp. 273–299.

Jop, S. (ed.) (2012). *Com'è bella l'imprudenza. Arti e teatri in rete: una cartografia dell'Italia che torna in scena.* Available online: http://www.lavoroculturale.org/imprudenza/ (Last accessed 15 June 2021).

Jørgensen, M. and Phillips, L. (2002). *Discourse Analysis as Theory and Method.* London: SAGE.

Juris, J. S. (2008). 'The New Digital Media and Activist Networking within Anti-Corporate Globalization Movements'. In J. X. Inda and R. Rosaldo (eds.), *The Anthropology of Globalization.* Malden, MA: Blackwell, pp. 352–70,

Juris, J. S. (2012). 'Reflections on #Occupy Everywhere: Social Media, Public Space, and Emerging Logics of Aggregation'. *American Ethnologist*, 39(2), pp. 259–279.

Katz, R. S. and Mair, P. (1995). 'Changing Models of Party Organization and Party Democracy: The Emergence of the Cartel Party'. *Party Politics*, 1(1), pp. 5–28.

Kavada, A. (2013). 'Internet Cultures and Protest Movements: The Cultural Links Between Strategy, Organizing and Online Communication'. In B. Cammerts, A. Mattoni and P. McCurdy (eds.), *Mediation and Protest Movements.* Chicago: The University of Chicago Press.

Kester, G. (2011). *The One and the Many: Contemporary Collaborative Art in a Global Context.* Durham, NC: Duke University Press.

Kirchberg, V. and Kagan, S. (2013). 'The Roles of Artists in the Emergence of Creative Sustainable Cities: Theoretical Clues and Empirical Illustrations'. *City, Culture and Society*, 4(3), pp. 137–152. doi: 10.1016/j.ccs.2013.04.001.

Kirchner, J. (2007). *Appeasing Bankers: Financial Caution on the Road to War.* Princeton, NJ: Princeton University Press.

Krätke, S. (2012). *The Creative Capital of Cities: Interactive Knowledge Creation and the Urbanization Economies of Innovation.* Hoboken, NJ: John Wiley & Sons.

Krause, S. R. (2008). *Civil Passions: Moral Sentiment and Democratic Deliberation.* Princeton: Princeton University Press.

Latour, B. and Weibel, P. (2005). *Making Things Public: Atmospheres of Democracy.* Cambridge: MIT Press.

Latour, B. (2005). *Reassembling the Social: An Introduction to Actor-Network-Theory.* Oxford: Oxford University Press.

Lazzarato, M. (1996). *Lavoro immateriale: forme di vita e produzione di soggettività.* Verona: Ombre corte.

Lazzarato, M. (2005). *La politica dell'evento.* Soveria Mannelli: Rubbettino.

Lazzarato, M. (2007). 'The Misfortunes of the "Artistic Critique" and of Cultural Employment', in *Transversal*, 1. Available online: http://eipcp.net/transversal/0207/lazzarato/en

Lazzarato, M. (2014). *Marcel Duchamp e il Rifiuto del Lavoro.* Milan: Edizioni Temporale.

Leslie, D. and Rantisi, N. M. (2011). 'Creativity and Place in the Evolution of a Cultural Industry'. *Urban Studies*, 48(9), pp. 1771–1787. doi: 10.1177/0042098010377475.

Lloyd, R. (2006). *Neo-Bohemia: Art and Commerce in the Postindustrial City*. New York: London: Routledge.

Lonzi, C. (1978). *Sputiamo su Hegel. La donna clitoridea e la donna vaginale e altri scritti.* Milan: Scritti di Rivolta Femminile.

Macao (2012a). *La Produzione Artistica E Culturale Nella Citta Fabbrica Sistemi Di Cattura E Pratiche Di Lotta*. Report. 1 December 2012. Italian. Available at: http://issuu.com/macaoMilan/docs/69300_ore (Accessed 15 March 2021).

Macao (2012b). Summer Camp diary, day two. Macao Website. Available at: http://www.macaoMilan.org/articoli/3190/macao-summer-camp-giorno-due (Accessed 01 January 2013).

Macao (2013). *Occupare il Conflitto*. Seminar, May 2013, Macao, the Exchange, Milan.

Macao (2014). *Macao Meets Workcenter of J Grotowski and T Richards*. Press kit. Italian. Available at: https://www.indiegogo.com/projects/macao-meets-workcenter-of-j-grotowski-t-richards (Accessed 16 March 2021).

MacKenzie D. and Wajcman, J. (1985). *The Social Shaping of Technology*. Milton Keynesand Philadelphia: Open University Press.

Mainsbridge, J. (1996). 'Using Power/Fighting Power: The Polity'. In S. Benhabib (ed.), *Democracy and Difference: Contesting the Boundaries of the Political.* Princeton, NJ: Princeton University Press, pp. 46–66.

Marcus, G. E. (1995). 'Ethnography in/of the World System: The Emergence of Multi-Sited Ethnography'. *Annual Review of Anthropology*, 24, pp. 95–117.

Mathieu, L. and Balasinski, J. (eds.) (2006). *Art et Contestation.* Rennes: Presses Universitaires des Rennes.

Mattei, U. (2011). *Beni Comuni. Un Manifesto*. Roma-Bari: Laterza.

Mattoni, A. (2012). *Media Practices and Protest Politics. How Precarious Workers Mobilise.* Farnham: Ashgate.

Mayer, M. (2009). 'The "Right to the City" in the Context of Shifting Mottos of Urban Social Movements'. *City*, 13(2–3), pp. 362–374. doi: 10.1080/13604810902982755.

Mayer, M. (2013). Preface, in 'Squatting Europe Kollective'. In *Squatting in Europe. Radical Spaces, Urban Struggles.* New York: Minor Compositions.

McBride, W. (1975). 'Marxism and Phenomenology'. *Journal of the British Society for Phenomenology*, 6(1), pp. 13–22.

McLean, H. E. (2014). 'Cracks in the Creative City: The Contradictions of Community Arts Practice'. *International Journal of Urban and Regional Research*, 38(6), 2156–2173. doi: 10.1111/1468-2427.12168.

McRobbie, A. (2011). 'Re-Thinking Creative Economy as Radical Social Enterprise. *Variant*, 41. Retrieved from http://www.variant.org.uk/41texts/amcrobbie41.html

Melucci, A. (1994). A Strange Kind of Newness: What's "New" in New Social Movements? In E. Larana, H. Jonhston H. and J. R. Gusfield (eds.), *New Social Movements: From Ideology to Identity*. Philadelphia: Temple University Press.

Melucci, A. (1996). *Challenging Codes. Collective Action in the Information Age*. Cambridge University Press, Cambridge.

Menger, P. M. (2001). 'Artists as Workers: Theoretical and Methodological Challenges'. *Poetics*, 28(4), pp. 241–254.

Mirzoeff, N. (ed.) (2013). *Militant Research Handbook*. New York: NYU Digital Publication. URL: http://steinhardt.nyu.edu/scmsAdmin/media/users/dhp238/Faculty_Projects/MRH_Web_SinglePage.pdf (Accessed 15 January 2015).

Moore, A. W. (2015). *Occupation culture. Art & Squatting in the City from Below*. New York: Minor Compositions.

Morini, C. and Vignola P. (2015). 'Introduzione'. In C. Morini and P. Vignola (eds.), *Piccola enciclopedia precaria: dai "Quaderni di San Precario"*. Milan: Agenzia X.

Moroni, P., Farina, D. and Tripodi, P. (1995). *Centri sociali: che impresa! Oltre il ghetto: un dibattito cruciale*. Roma: Castelvecchi.

Mouffe, C. (1999). 'Deliberative Democracy or Agonistic Pluralism?' *Social Research*, 66(3), pp. 745–758.

Negri, A. (1992). *Marx Beyond Marx*. London: Pluto Press.

Negri, A. (2009). 'Arte e lavoro immateriale'. In M. Baravalle (ed.), *L'arte della Sovversione. Multiversity: pratiche artistiche contemporanee e attivisimo politico*. Rome: Manifestolibri.

Neilson, B. and Rossiter, N. (2008). 'Precarity as a Political Concept, or, Fordism as Exception'. *Theory, Culture and Society*, 25(7–8), pp. 51–72. doi: 10.1177/0263276408097796.

Niessen, B. (2009). *Going commercial. L'integrazione degli artisti underground a Milan e Berlino*. (PhD Thesis). University of Milan – Bicocca.

Novy, J. and Colomb, C. (2013). 'Struggling for the Right to the (Creative) City in Berlin and Hamburg: New Urban Social Movements, New "Spaces of Hope"?' *International Journal of Urban and Regional Research*, 37(5), pp. 1816–1838.

Nunes, R. (2014). *Organization of the Organizationless: Collective Action after Networks*. London: Mute Books & Post-Media Lab.

OECD, (2011). *Divided We Stand: Why Inequality Keeps Rising*. OECD Report 2011.

Papacharissi, Z. (2010). A *Private Sphere. Democracy in a Digital Age*. Cambridge: Polity Press.

Peck, J. (2005). 'Struggling with the Creative Class'. *International Journal of Urban and Regional Research*, 29(4), pp. 740–770.

Perniola, M. (1998). *I Situazionisti: il movimento che ha profetizzato la "società dello spettacolo"*. Roma: Castelvecchi.

Pradel, M. and Martì-Costa, M. (2012). 'The Knowledge City Against Urban Creativity? Artists' Workshops and Urban Regeneration in Barcelona'. *European Urban and Regional Studies*, 19(1), pp. 92–108.

Pratt, A. C. (2008). 'Creative Cities: The Cultural Industries and the Creative Class'. *Geografiska annaler: Series B - Human geography*, 90(2), pp. 107–117.

Pratt, A. C. (2011). 'The Cultural Contradictions of the Creative City'. *City, Culture and Society*, 2(3), pp. 123–130. doi: 10.1016/j.ccs.2011.08.00

Privitera, W. (2001). *Sfera pubblica e democratizzazione*. Rome-Bari: Laterza.

Pruijt, H. (2004). 'Squatters in the Creative City: Rejoinder to Justus Uitermark'. *International Journal of Urban and Regional Research*, 28(3), pp. 699–705. doi: 10.1111/j.0309-1317.2004.00544.x.

Pruijt, H. (2013). 'The Logic of Urban Squatting'. *International Journal of Urban and Regional Research*, 37(1), 19–45. doi: 10.1111/j.1468-2427.2012.01116.x

Putnam, R. D. (1993). *Making Democracy Work.* Princeton University Press.

Rancière, J. (2007). *Hatred of Democracy.* London: Verso.

Reed, T. V. (2005). *The Art of Protest: Culture and Activism from the Civil Rights Movement to the Streets of Seattle.* Minneapolis, MN: University of Minnesota Press.

Reed-Danahay, D. (1997). Introduction. In D. Reed-Danahay (ed.), *Auto/Ethnography: Rewriting the Self and the Social.* Oxford: Berg.

Renault, M. and Sibertin-Blanc, G. (2018). 'Se réapproprier Spinoza: Usages et mésusages d'un philosophe à la mode'. *Revue du Crieur*, 2(2), pp. 144–159. doi: 10.3917/crieu.010.0144.

Rieder, B. (2013). 'Studying Facebook via Data Extraction: The Netvizz Application'. In *WebSci '13 Proceedings of the 5th Annual ACM Web Science Conference*, pp. 346–355. doi: 10.1145/2464464.2464475.

Rogers, R. (2013). *Digital Methods.* Cambridge, MA.: Mit Press.

Rosanvallon, P. (2006). *La contre-démocratie. La politique à l'âge de la défiance.* Paris: Seuil.

Rosler, M. (2010). 'Culture Class: Art, Creativity, Urbanism, Part I', *E-Flux*, Issue no. 21, 12/2010.

Sabatini, F. (2005). 'Un atlante del capitale sociale italiano'. *Terzo Forum Annuale per Giovani Ricercatori*, Bologna.

Serafini, P., Holtaway, J. and Cossu, A. (eds.) (2017). *artWORK: Art, Labour and Activism.* London: Rowman & Littlefield.

Sewell, W. H. (1996). 'Three Temporalities: Toward an Eventful Sociology'. In T. J. McDonald (ed.), *The Historic Turn in the Human Sciences.* Ann Arbor, MI: University of Michigan Press.

Sherwood Festival (2021). Festival Webpage. Italian. Available at: http://www.sherwood.it/festival (Accessed 15 March 2021).

Shifman, L. (2012). 'An Anatomy of a YouTube Meme'. *New Media and Society*, 14(2), pp. 187–203.

Sholette, G. (2011). *Dark Matter: Art and Politics in the Age of Enterprise Culture.* London: Pluto Press.

Sholette, G. (2016). 'Merciless Aesthetic: Activist Art as the Return of Institutional Critique. A Response to Boris Groys.' *Field*, 4(2021). Available at: http://field-journal.com/issue-4/merciless-aesthetic-activist-art-as-the-return-of-institutional-critique-a-response-to-boris-groys (Last Access 30 June 2021).

Skinner, Q. (1986). *Ambrogio Lorenzetti: The Artist as Political Philosopher.* Raileigh Lecture on History, Proceedings of the British Academy, 72, pp. 1–56.

Snow, D. (2001). 'Analyse des cadres des mouvements sociaux'. In D. Cefai and D. Trom (eds.), *Les formes de l'action collective.* Paris: Editions EHESS, pp. 27–49.

Snricek, N. and Williams, A. (2016). *Inventing the Future: Postcapitalism and a World Without Work.* London: Verso.

Sparti, D. (2002). *Epistemologia delle Scienze Sociali.* Bologna: Mulino.

Squatting Europe Kollective. (2013). *Squatting in Europe. Radical Spaces, Urban Struggles.* New York: Minor Compositions.

Starr, A. Fernandez, L. and Scholl, C. (2011). *Shutting Down the Streets: Political Violence and Social Control in the Global Era*. New York: New York University Press.

Steiner, J. (2012). *The Foundations of Deliberative Democracy*. Cambridge: Cambridge University Press.

Steiner, J., Bachtiger, A., Sporndli, M. and Steenberger, M. R. (2004). *Deliberative Politics in Action. Analysing Parliamentary Discourse*. Cambridge: Cambridge University Press.

Swann T. and Stoborod K. (2014). 'Did You Hear About the Anarchist Manager?' *Ephemera Journal*, 14(4), pp. 591–609.

Tarrow, S. (1989). *Democracy and Disorder: Protest and Politics in Italy, 1965-1975*. Oxford: Clarendon Press.

Tarrow, S. (1998). *Power in Movement: Collective Action, Social Movements and Politics*. Cambridge University Press.

Tilly, C. (1986). *The Contentions French*. Cambridge, MA: Harvard University Press.

Tilly, C. and Tarrow, S. (2007). *Contentious Politics*. Boulder, CO: Paradigm.

Todd, E. (2008). *Après la démocratie*. Paris: Gallimard.

Tronti, M. (1966). *Operai e Capitale (Workers and Capital)*. Turin: Einaudi.

Tucker, K. H. (2012). *Workers of the World Enjoy. Aesthetic Politics from Revolutionary Syndicalism to the Global Justice Movement*. Philadelphia: Temple University Press.

Uitermark, J. (2004). 'The Co-optation of Squatters in Amsterdam and the Emergence of a Movement Meritocracy: A Critical Reply to Pruijt'. *International Journal of Urban and Regional Research*, 28(3), pp. 687–698. doi: 10.1111/j.0309-1317.2004.00543.x

UNDP (2011). *United Nations Human Development, Report 2011*.

Valli, C. (2015). 'When Cultural Workers Become an Urban Social Movement. Political subjectification and alternative cultural production in the Macao movement, Milan'. *Environment and Planning A*.

Vicari Haddock, S. (2010). 'Branding the Creative City'. In S. Vicari Haddock (ed.), *Brand-Building: The Creative City. A Critical Look at Current Concepts and Practices*. Florence, Italy: Florence University Press.

Vivant, E. (2009). 'How Underground Culture is Changing Paris'. *Urban Research and Practice*, 2(1).

Vivant, E. (2013). 'Creatives in the City: Urban Contradictions of the Creative City'. *City, Culture and Society*, 4(2), pp. 57–63. doi: 10.1016/j.ccs.2013.02.003.

Weber, M. (2019). *Economy and Society: A New Translation*. London: Harvard University Press.

Weibel, P. (ed.) (2015). *Global Activism: Art and Conflict in the 21st Century*. Cambridge, MA and London: The MIT Press.

Western, S. (2015). 'Autonomist Leadership in Leaderless Movements: Anarchists Leading the Way'. *Ephemera Journal*, 14(4), pp. 673–698.

Whybrow, N. (2011). *Art and the City*. London: I. B. Tauris.

Young, I. M. (2003). 'Activist Challenges to Deliberative Democracy'. In J. S. Fishkin and P. Laslett (eds.), *Debating Deliberative Democracy*. Malden, MA: Blackwell, pp. 102–120.

Zamponi, L. (2012). 'Why Don't Italians Occupy?' *Hypotheses on a Failed Mobilisation, Social Movement Studies,* 11(3–4), pp. 416–426.
Zamponi, L. (2018). *Social Movements, Memory and Media: Narrative in Action in the Italian and Spanish Student Movements*. London: Palgrave.
Žižek, S. (2012). *The Year of Dreaming Dangerously*. London: Verso.
Zukin, S. (1989). *Loft Living: Culture and Capital in Urban Change*. New Brusnwick, NJ: Rutgers University Press.
Zukin, S. (1991). *Landscapes of Power: From Detroit to Disney World.* Berkeley: University of California Press.

# Index

Note. Page locators in italics refer to figures.